I. COMPTON-BURNETT

I. COMPTON-BURNETT

by

CHARLES BURKHART

LONDON
VICTOR GOLLANCZ LTD
1965

PRINTED IN GREAT BRITAIN
BY EBENEZER BAYLIS AND SON, LTD.
THE TRINITY PRESS, WORCESTER, AND LONDON

ACKNOWLEDGMENTS

I am grateful to Temple University for grants of time and money, and for other aid, in the form of personal and patient advice, from Professors Elisabeth W. Schneider, Mabel P. Worthington, and William K. Rose. Mr. Charles R. McDonald helped me greatly in the editing. Miss Kay Dick was a most valuable consultant. Mr. Herman Schrijver was my literary arbiter in more matters than I could name; and Miss I. Compton-Burnett has, over a period of years, proved what kindness is.

FOR

HERMAN SCHRIJVER

CONTENTS

I. COMPTON-BURNETT

CHAPTER ONE

TOWARDS A DEFINITION OF THE ECCENTRIC NOVEL

"What seems beautiful to me, what I should like to write, is a book about nothing."

—Flaubert, in a letter to Louise Colet, January 16, 1852.

One of the dangers of adjectives is that there are not very many of them. The adjectives in English are more threadbare than its verbs: and in general English seems a language worn smooth, one in which the individual word has been replaced by the phrase, which itself has become an automatic unit, a rehearsed response. In reading a page of English prose of any century before our own, one feels an immediate relation between the writer and his diction, an alert and vital closeness; but a curious sense of distance can strike us in reading a page of modern prose, whether newspaper or novel: the impression that blocs of words are being used deafly, like counters in a game, the "communications game"—mechanically and conventionally shuffled in a variety of familiar patterns. Adjectives are likely victims, whether in literary criticism which overuses the word "great" or in the advertisement of a "colossal" new film. And of course it has always been far easier work for a writer to describe an action, with adjectives, than to dramatize it, with verbs, and with the real rhythms of passionate and heightened speech.

It is particularly the adjectives which connote approval that have become flimsy and fatigued. Advertising is one of the typical arts of our age; and since it is a noisy age, there is a sustained shout of superlatives for every new product, whether of the literary imagination or of a soap manufacturer. On the dust jackets of their books, all writers are praised; because the "soft sell" has not yet reached the publishing world, the same tired troop ("remarkable," "powerful," "stirring," and so on) are deployed for every first novel about sensitive adolescence, every raw and wriggling specimen of neo-romantic neo-brutalism. The babble of adjectives is sustained at such intensity, especially in America, that it tends to move right out of the range of human hearing. It is charity to suppose that this was the intention.

Whatever the value of adjectives today, those that praise and those that don't, there is, all the same, something remarkable in the degree of praise accorded the author whose works are the subject of the present study—an author whose style is the opposite of adjectival, and who has stood far aside from those massive cultural conformisms of which the decline of language is only the sign. The dust jackets do for once represent what is usually said of her novels by exact and discriminating critics, whose reviews do not succumb to the temptation of either the perfunctory or the malicious: what is usually said, and what has been said for nearly forty years. Most critics would agree that Ivy Compton-Burnett is "probably the purest and most original of contemporary English artists" (Rosamond Lehmann) and a "remarkable and unusual novelist, who has, in her own well-tilled field, no rival and no parallel" (*The Times Literary Supplement*); that her novels are "unique in style and content" (Phyllis Bentley) and that they are "conceived on the same moral and intellectual level as those of Henry James" (Edward Sackville-West).

What unfavourable criticism there has been has sometimes accused the author of preciosity and her admirers of coterie. Charges of "decadence," "amorality," and the like have been made. A tone of respectful and polite bewilderment has also been heard. But her fellow-novelists—she is a writer's writer, if ever there was one—have been her best critics, and there is not much dissent among them. What there is, I hope to comment on. Generally, they credit her with extraordinary accomplishment. In my own opinion, in comparison with her writing most other modern writing seems unfinished, its aim diffuse and its style impure.

With all the enthusiasm that critics have shown and with the inevitable references to her work that any discussion of the modern novel includes, the question that must often have occurred to admirers of these novels is the simple one: why, then, aren't they much more widely read? They have a steady sale, and a "growing band of admirers" is often spoken of, but only *Manservant and Maidservant* (1947), I should think, has approached the status of best seller. Writers with far less favourable reviews—I mean literary writers, not hacks—command far larger sales. And we have welcomed a wondrous diversity of writers in recent times; Burroughs has sold his thousands, and Kerouac his tens of thousands. In the face of so maintained and brilliant an achievement as the eighteen novels from *Pastors and Masters* (1925) to *A God and his Gifts* (1963), why have they missed an easy general acceptance?

It is not, as one hears said, because the novels are not easy. In the year 1911, *Dolores* was published. This was Miss Compton-Burnett's first and atypical novel which neither critics nor Miss Compton-Burnett herself considers part of the canon of her work. Regardless of its merit, however, this first work was published in the same year as Lawrence's first novel, *The White Peacock*, a fact that can induce reflection; *Death in Venice* was published in that year; only two years later the first volume of Proust's huge work appeared: we have taken readily enough, after only a few years of absorption, to difficulties as diverse as *Ulysses*, *The Waste Land*, *The Metamorphosis*, *The Stranger*, and *The Comedian as the Letter C*. In this century such writers as Joyce and Kafka begin with a small band of devotees; the devotees go forth and teach all nations; Joyce and Kafka become standard authors whom every university student talks about, and may even have read (unless they have begun to seem old-fashioned to him, and he has discovered Genet and Beckett). But with some authors, why does the band of devotees harden into coterie, never become, if not an army, at least something more than a household word heard only in the palace of art? One hears said also that these novels are too narrow, that they do not appeal to an accessible and sufficient range of human experience. But it would be very strange to say this of Miss Compton-Burnett's novels, since they concern the family, and everyone has a family.

A definition of the eccentric novel is difficult. For one thing, the name itself apparently contradicts the possibility of definition: eccentric novels are as different from one another as they are different from novels that aren't called eccentric. Yet the term exists. One thinks of Peacock. One has to think of the term in connection with Miss Compton-Burnett's novels because it has so frequently been made a convenient label for them. Labels often serve as a kind of escape from definition; but one definition that seems to lie behind the use of the term is essentially a quantitative one: an eccentric writer is a writer of extreme individuality whose audience has remained small. The problem of a more workable and specific definition is complicated by the fact that every novelist is an eccentric novelist in the sense that every writer has his own tone. Virginia Woolf is as characteristic of herself as Hemingway is characteristic of himself. On the lowest level, writers have hardly any individual tone (although I do not know that it is true that the higher the level the more individual—and therefore, in a sense, the more eccentric—the tone). A writer without his own tone is no writer at all.

Every writer is eccentric in the larger sense that he has his solitary vision, a world of his own, an unique geography of the imagination. In 1949 V. S. Pritchett wrote about the state of the novel:

> . . . If we have stood still for the fourteen years since the Spanish Civil War I think we have not been idle. We have been most diligently and searchingly revising the ordinary material of the novel. From this documentary soil I prophesy that we shall shortly grow the great eccentric and romantic blooms which are in our tradition. . . .[1]

Dickens is one such "great eccentric and romantic" novelist, as is Sterne, or Hardy, or Lawrence. It is helpful to keep in mind this sense of the word eccentric and its implications in our attempt to deduce that narrower or deeper sense which may be of value in placing the novels of Miss Compton-Burnett.

To me the word eccentric, used in the latter sense, does not mean minor. Nor does it, on the other hand, mean something which is in some way better than the non-eccentric: Peacock may be a better or a worse writer than Ouida, but not because he is eccentric and she, except (once again) in the sense that all writers are, is not. Indeed criticism should not rate but illuminate. The busy awarding of a varying number of gold stars is, at least in my opinion, a pious but elementary practice. Miss Compton-Burnett's books may be "better" or "worse" than those of Graham Greene; if we were to decide, it is not the decision itself that would be profitable, but the reasons for it that, hopefully, would be, since they would increase our enjoyment of her writing. In short, the word eccentric is for us a *modus operandi* and not in itself a critical judgment. And if the word is useful at all, it is useful relatively rather than absolutely—that is, every writer is more or less eccentric, in one or more aspects distant from some imaginary centre of the novel.

There is, I think, somewhere in the mind of every novel-reader, an idea of what a novel is like. This idea, which may be quite unformed and unconscious, is the product of all the novels that he has read. It is a synthesis of his experiences in the novelistic domain, even, perhaps, of all the narrative he has ever heard or read, from nursery tales to newspaper accounts; and from this synthesis he derives his expectations of what the new novel that he picks up to read will be like. Though the novel as a form escapes precise definition, it would seem that the novel-reader's expectations are still largely based, even today, on the immensely popular novels of the Victorians, from the Brontës to Hardy—read, and read again, as they still are.

No one, however, wants only echoes. Angela Thirkell is too imitative of Trollope. The new novel must be new, if the novel-reader is to enjoy it; that is, it must add to and alter his entire residual concept of the novel at the same time that it must appeal to and gratify his sense of the novelistically familiar, the fictionally habitual. A novel must be new and not new. One definition of the eccentric novel might be that it disappoints this delicate balance of expectation in the reader's mind by offering too much that is new, too little of the old conventions of psychology and morality and action. The eccentric novelist offers his new wares all at once, he begins by being what he is, and he remains it, he is static; the non-eccentric takes us with him step by step, he develops, he progresses from the new/old *Dubliners* and *Portrait of the Artist as a Young Man* until he climbs the last peak—and here he may have left most of us behind, gasping in the thin air where, we protest, our literary expectations are no longer sufficiently nourished—of *Finnegans Wake*. The late novels of the usual novelist may or may not be as good as his early novels: my point is that they are not the same.

To move from the reader to the writer—to move from our reactions as readers, which are, at least sometimes, observable, to the hidden creative process of the artist himself—is to involve us more deeply in the speculative and the deductive. To consider the distinctions between the creative process of the eccentric writer and that of the non-eccentric writer, we shall make use of two notions or ideas which apply to all writing and, I believe, to all art. Both are familiar ideas, and both are controversial. They concern the relationships of the artist with himself and with the world.

The first is that art arises from obsession. The second is that the condition of art reflects the condition of the world.

Obsession is a dramatic word, and a word that has been a little lowered by its status as psychological jargon. It may not be the right word here. But the idea can be stated simply: it is not placidity that produces art, it is need that does. However, everyone has obsessions, and artists are uncommon. A writer must also have the gifts of energy, intelligence, and observation. Yet behind these gifts, or underneath them, is the obsession that must and will be heard, and upon which a writer's gifts are employed to impose a bearable constraint. This constraint is called form. Form discovers itself again and again as the flower unfolding, but it is the dark roots that have pushed the flower into the sun. It is easier to see that Dostoevsky was obsessed than that Mrs. Gaskell was. But both were.

The eccentric writer is more governed by his obsessions than either Dostoevsky or Mrs. Gaskell, and must in turn govern them more. Therefore his books tend to be more like one another than other writers' books are; they give an impression of sameness. Also, there is less development, development in any sense—in vision, in power, in purpose. There is less experimentation, and there is less shape and pattern to the *œuvre* of such writers. The form of their work is unusually pronounced and distinctive, even obviously rigid, since their need for controlling their need is greater than that of other writers. Not for them the expansive sprawl of Thackeray or the garrulous intensity of Lawrence. Once again I do not intend to suggest an arbitrary or exclusive classification here or elsewhere: many a writer not primarily eccentric has one or more of the characteristics just described (for example, Thomas Wolfe seems to me to have written the same book several times, and the form of Corneille's plays is "unusually pronounced and distinctive"). I wish only to suggest that the obsession—the need, creative trauma, or whatever one wishes to call it—plays a more nearly visible part in the work of the eccentric writer. Nor do I wish to try to make it even more visible in the present case by speculation about the author's life. The perils of biographical criticism are as justly celebrated as its irrelevancies. Moreover it is usually impertinent to inquire into the life of living authors; even, sometimes, of dead ones. It is enough to say that the subjects to which Miss Compton-Burnett has returned again and again must have their origin in events of her early life, and that they are very deeply rooted there.

The other concept important to these distinctions is that the condition of art reflects the condition of the world. The artist derives his decorums, those that attempt to render serene his obsessions, from the world, as the world is acted upon by his imagination. The gesture of withdrawal from the world, in Byzantine disdain to enter into an ivory tower, is in itself an attitude towards the world. Ideally, the process of art is one in which the artist's vision of the world is returned to the world and becomes its vision of itself, a symbiotic enrichment.

In our own time there has been a decline in this two-way communication between the artist and his audience, commented upon to the extent that it has become a cliché of literary/social history. With the fragmentation of our culture, art has become more nearly hermetic (it can never be entirely so), and our poets talk to themselves. For an example of the communication that once prevailed, one thinks of Dickens' day and Edgar Johnson's account of the serial publication of *The Old Curiosity Shop*: "Waiting crowds at a New York pier shouted to an incoming vessel, 'Is Little Nell dead?' "[2] The best seller of today is seldom on a literary level; for one di Lampedusa *Leopard* there are a dozen *Peyton Places*. So many historical causes have been given for this cultural schism; one wonders if the most basic is not the simplest: there are so many more people in the world today.

The eccentric novel has always been more shut off from the world that we have agreed to call real. The consequence is that it bears a less familiar resemblance to the outer world, though not necessarily a less meaningful one. We are confined to the world of the eccentric novel in such a way that the daily stridencies of the other world are muted, and we may feel that we are in a hothouse rather than on the open road of the imagination. Firbank is a good example of the eccentric novelist's relationship with the external world, some aspects of which in him have undergone a sea change, an alchemy—have been refracted cubistically: and become that bizarre kingdom where Queen Thleeanouhee of the Land of Dates is a welcome guest. George Moore is an interesting example of a writer whose late novels begin to take on eccentric characteristics. With that particular mixture of naïveté and profundity which marked his long career, he sensed his age, and rejected it. In a letter of 1917, he wrote, "I abhor the modern idea that literature is written for everybody and sent round with the modern loaf and the milk up to standard."[3] In 1916 he had begun to publish his books in limited editions, creating, for the title-page of these late private-press works, Cumann Seaneolais na h'Eireann, the Society for Irish Folklore. His late novels, beginning with *The Brook Kerith* in 1916, are set in remote times and places—*Héloïse and Abelard, Ulick and Soracha, Aphrodite in Aulis.*

Miss Compton-Burnett has said, "I do not feel that I have any real or organic knowledge of life later than about 1910."[4] Her created world has been an English country house. It is in or near a village. The date, when stated, is, at the earliest, 1885 (*A House and its Head*), and at the latest, 1901 (*A Family and a Fortune*). There are one or more nearby houses, sometimes a shop or two. One feels that the village is in the South of England. London is mentioned, as are lands across the seas, though the latter almost never by name: external geography is used only as a plot device, there are places to which people go and from which they return, but the walls of the country house confine us together with her talkative family. One becomes an inhabitant entirely at home, although the home is not a comfortable one in any sense. No novelist has more rigorously excluded the external world, more intensely posited the world of her imagination.

Yet, because there is a tyrant in this home, critics have been tempted to find some relationship between his tyranny and those massive tyrannies which have disfigured the face of our century. Miss Compton-Burnett has herself lent some support to the possibility: "When war casts its shadow, I find that I recoil," she once said.[5] Edward Sackville-West has written, "Apart from physical violence and starvation, there is no feature of the totalitarian régime which has not its counterpart in the atrocious families depicted in these books."[6] Miss Compton-Burnett's statement in a recent interview is also relevant:

> INTERVIEWER: . . . It has been suggested that despite the setting of your novels, the forces presented in them, particularly those that emerge as domestic tyranny, are precisely those which on a larger scale have recently produced wars and revolutions and totalitarian régimes. Have you thought about that?
>
> MISS COMPTON-BURNETT: No, I've never thought of it, but I think that the things that do produce such troubles probably are those forces. The same that produce them on a small scale in ordinary life. The sweep of them on a great scale would lead to that sort of tragedy.[7]

That she had "never thought of it" shows that whatever her novels might appear to mirror of "wars and revolutions and totalitarian régimes," the reflection must be quite an unconscious one. The isolation and other features of her fictional world suggest that her imagination does not respond to the political, the historical, the sociological; I am inclined to believe that the parallels of tyranny which have been found between her work and our history are fortuitous, unrecognized even unconsciously. It is easier to forget in her novels that the contemporary world exists than it is in any other novels one can think of, eccentric or otherwise.

From these two fundamental traits, that the eccentric novelist is more ordered by his obsession and that the world he has made is more private a place—which are in fact but one trait, since the second is the result of the first—from these, stem a variety of other characteristics. As we said earlier, an eccentric novelist tends to begin with the originality that other writers grow into. Once the pattern foreshadowed in *Pastors and Masters* (1925) had become clarified in the next novel, *Brothers and Sisters* (1929), it was not much altered. What few changes there have been will be discussed later.

Because of their originality the novels of Miss Compton-Burnett do not invite a study of their "literary influences." One could not say (if one wanted to) of an eccentric novel, "in the naturalistic tradition" or "influenced by Hemingway" or "novel of sensibility"; it springs full-grown from the head of its creator. Comparisons, however, have often been made (and often confused with influences) between Miss Compton-Burnett and other writers. She stands alone, although she has been compared to Jane Austen, most of all; and for some reason—is it an impression of excessive artifice?—to Henry James; and to the Greek, Elizabethan, and Jacobean dramatists; to Mrs. Gaskell, persuasively, by Edward Sackville-West; to Congreve and Wilde; to Samuel Butler and Nathalie Sarraute; and to Mrs. Henry de la Pasture, by Evelyn Waugh.

Nor do the eccentrics inspire imitation. One occasionally hears a line or two of Compton-Burnett dialogue in the work of a younger author; for example there are traces of her influence in William Trevor's novel of 1964, *The Old Boys*. The critic Bernard McCabe has called Nathalie Sarraute a "notable 'objectivist' disciple" of Miss Compton-Burnett; but no matter what admiration Miss Sarraute has expressed for what she conceives to be the intent of Miss Compton-Burnett's dialogue, both the surface and the substrata of her novels are, I should say, very different indeed from Miss Compton-Burnett's.[8] One can summarize the unlikelihood of the influence of Miss Compton-Burnett's work being felt at all widely among other novelists by saying arbitrarily that Shakespeare is the least eccentric of writers, and that he has had the most influence.

The tone of the eccentric writer is so highly individual that it inspires parody more readily than imitation. Occasionally he sounds as if he is talking to himself, a soliloquy in his shut-off world. Frances Newman—an American eccentric writer whose novels are at present forgotten—has so baroque a style that she sometimes sounds as if she is parodying herself. Dickens sounds like Dickens, but not to the extent that Firbank sounds like Firbank. Still, all writers sound like themselves, as we pointed out above, and it is only this quality of soliloquy, of incantatory self-absorption, of the voice turned and tuned inward rather than outward, that one can instance as a trait, if only a minor one, of the eccentric.

Generally speaking, the English novel has been morally *engagé*; it has been didactic; it has had its masterpieces of social protest; it has preached and prayed; it has had the liveliest concern with conduct, both social and personal. A major difference of the eccentric novel is that it has never been a novel of social protest, or in fact of social anything, because its imagined milieu is more divorced or remote from an actual environment both in its geography and in its lack of a sharp contemporaneity, and because it is turned inward rather than outward. It may be said that Peacock's novels are full of the things of his age—but how tidy and objective his satire is, from how placid a distance he regards the people he satirizes, like Scythrop and Mr. Flosky, in comparison with, for example, Swift, feverish in the land of the Houyhnhnms. In the French novel the example of Flaubert is instructive. The essential and productive tension in Flaubert, the great proponent of objectivity, is between the objectivity he tried with so much intelligence to practise, and the romantic impulse which was his nature and his heritage; between his scorn of the bourgeois of the July Monarchy like Homais, and his hope, his tragic imagination, of the hero and the heroic. In this as in many ways Flaubert is the epitome of the modern artist, and his struggle is theirs. "Judge not," was his motto, but he could not help judging. The detachment at which he aimed, the superb indifference with which he sought to observe, to record, and to refrain from comment, is the eccentric novelist's natural endowment. Two modern writers in English who seem to me genuinely objective are James Joyce, from *Ulysses* on (though it is in the *Portrait* that Stephen gives his famous definition: "The artist, like the God of the creation, remains within or behind or beyond or above his handiwork, invisible, refined out of existence, indifferent, paring his fingernails") and Miss Compton-Burnett, who may deal in moral matters, but who preaches no lesson, makes no comment, and offers no romantic hope.

In the quotation from V. S. Pritchett given above, the assumption is that the English novel is romantic. Eccentric novels can also be romantic, like Beckford's *Vathek* or Miss Newman's *Dead Lovers Are Faithful Lovers,* but nothing sets Miss Compton-Burnett's novels more distinctly to one side; they are unique in that between them and the romantic novel a great gulf is fixed. It is not that her novels are too much alike, not that they are difficult or strange, but that they are profoundly alien to the romantic tradition of the English novel. Empathy, identification, catharsis: these are the psychological commitments or involvements which the spectator or reader of a romantic work experiences far more vitally than the spectator or reader of a classical work. One does not like to use terms like romantic and classical loosely, nor does one like to question Aristotle: but one wonders how vital actually is the catharsis which the audience of the classical *King Oedipus* undergoes. I believe that it is greatly different in degree as well as in kind from the catharsis of the romantic *King Lear.* The fates of Miss Compton-Burnett's characters move one contemplatively, in the Greek manner. Her characters lack the mythic elements and proportions of Sophocles'; they are psychologically more complex than his—more Euripidean than Sophoclean; they are treated with a more persuasive and personal irony, though she never appeals to the sentiments even to the extent that Sophocles does. Probably the only romantic element of any kind that one could find in her works is her recourse to certain characteristics of the plots of romantic melodramas. The "melting mood" which Dickens and others of the Victorians attempted to capture through so many hundreds of their pages is utterly foreign to her; it is an iron eye that observes that family, in its chilly late-Victorian home.

The scope of the novel in its brief history has gradually dwindled, like an inverted pyramid. From the panorama of *Tom Jones,* to the little landscape of *Molloy*; from the broad statement, sociological and psychological and theological, to the cabbage-counting of Pinget or Robbe-Grillet. The old novel, with its pronouncedly sociological bias, attempted to sum up a cross-section of the external world in its internal world, and in that respect it was always allegorical; its grasp was so comprehensive that it could re-create the world in terms of Vanity Fair or the island of Lilliput. It spoke in the tone of a literate and humane man to an audience composed of similar men about concerns which speaker and audience had in common. The audience has wandered off in all directions, most of them into that vast and dismal no-man's-land which bears the contradictory name of popular culture. The new novel is perplexed to find even "fit audience though few," and far from surveying mankind with extensive view, it essays only the detailed exploration, whether sociological or psychological, of a detail—the world of junkies or the world of dreams. In the old novel, a village could be the microcosm of people and of a world; but the emphasis in the new novel is typically on the fugitive and aberrant personality, on a splinter group: since who can grasp, or who would want to try to grasp, the whole? Even if one could fit the fragments together they would remain a puzzle. And the tone has lost its exhortatory and confidential quality. We are too negative, too little sure of meanings, to commit ourselves to allegory.

The characteristics of the eccentric novel which have been here suggested may be the characteristics of the novel of the future. The novel about nothing which Flaubert said that he wished to write would be the purely eccentric novel, a novel, as he said, "which would be held together by the strength of its style, just as the earth, suspended in the void, depends on nothing external for its support." He added, "I believe that the future of Art lies in this direction." Flaubert's ideal novel would abandon altogether the hopeless task of explaining a world it never made, and which it could not translate into fictional terms; cast loose from the bewildering shore, it would float on the real seas of the imagination. The novel, which in the past was a kind of public testimony, would become private. Writers today whose work points towards the future include the novelists of the *nouvelle vague* in France, and they include Samuel Beckett and Ivy Compton-Burnett.

CHAPTER TWO

CONVENTIONS

"Books are very like plants. They are better, the more they are weeded, and they come up out of each other and are all the same."
—*Daughters and Sons*

I

WHAT THE CONVENTIONS ARE

Miss Compton-Burnett's novels have much in common with one another, far more than most writers' have. They have appeared fairly regularly at two- or three-year intervals, and the titles themselves have had a gnomic, often alliterative familiarity as novel has followed novel. Each title has told us something about the contents of the novel—*Brothers and Sisters*, for example, has six sets of brothers and sisters in it (the eldest pair of whom are also man and wife), while *A Family and a Fortune* concerns the effects of a large and unexpected inheritance which a dependent member of the household receives. In general the titles are not interchangeable, although *Men and Wives*, the climax of which is the murder of Harriet Haslam by her son Matthew, could with equal aptness, it would seem, be called *Mother and Son*, and *Mother and Son*, which is in part an account of courtship among certain middle-aged and elderly people, might almost as well be called *Men and Wives*.

Such similarities as exist among the titles are multiplied when we come to the novels proper. These similarities are what is initially most striking about the novels—similarities of mechanics and subject, what might be called veneer: what the novels look like. Every novelist adopts a set of conventions to serve as vehicle for his meaning—he chooses his settings, his point of view, characters, etc.—or, more accurately in most cases, they choose him. Miss Compton-Burnett's set of conventions varies much less from novel to novel than do other novelists'; to find a parallel, one would have to go to the drama, particularly the neo-classic drama, whether French or English, or perhaps the *pièce bien faite* of the late nineteenth century in France and in England. She has said of her work that it is "something between a novel and a play."[1] It is bare in texture, lacking, as Cecily Mackworth has said, "le bric-à-brac du roman traditionnel."[2] What I should like to outline here, more statistically than critically, is the typical novel/play of Miss Compton-Burnett, to summarize what the books look like, to condense, as it were, the eighteen books from *Pastors and Masters* to *A God and his Gifts* into a single book.

In Chapter I were already mentioned the setting, an English country house; the date of the events, roughly 1885–1900; the subject, family life. An American reviewer once wrote that a Compton-Burnett family is "about the size of a regiment."[3] Among them half-brothers and half-sisters are common, as are step-parents; the former often the result of an illegitimate union. There are illegitimate offspring in ten of the eighteen novels; illegitimacy is thematically most important in *Mother and Son*, a study of the powerful natural love a parent feels for his natural child and the child feels for him.

The household usually has its employees both above and below-stairs—a governess, a tutor, a nursemaid; a butler, a cook, a housemaid or two, a youthful footman. The later the novel, the more servants there are. The household invariably has its neighbours, one or more nearby families who flock to the central house on all urgent occasions and some that aren't; much of the rest of the time they spend in gossiping about it. The situation recalls Pirandello: a central family group, among whom the passions struggle, and a concentric group of outsiders, who comment like a chorus.

The attraction which the central household exercises is also shown by a pattern in some of the novels of outsiders attempting to merge with the principal family by marriage, an attempt which in almost all cases fails: it is as if the family were too occupied with one another for an outsider to claim any permanent attention. The best example is *Brothers and Sisters*, where Andrew Stace and his sister Caroline are left together at the end of the novel while some of their former matrimonial prospects, other sets of brothers and sisters, marry among themselves.

The first quarter of the novel, occupied with the introduction of characters, may seem static if one expects the wheels of plot to begin turning. We meet the characters fairly rapidly. Perhaps we meet them too rapidly in *A House and its Head*, where the five people introduced in Chapter I are joined by thirteen others in Chapter II: the result is that two or three of the thirteen are never quite so vivid as they were probably conceived, although it should be added that almost all the characters are recapitulated in Chapter III, where a foggy and pious lady named Beatrice Fellowes visits each household in turn "to bring once again," as she fatuously declares, "the simple message of Christmas . . . I feel we cannot give or receive the message too often."

At the time of his first appearance or shortly thereafter each character is briefly described. These descriptions vary in value. They can be as laconic and unhelpful as the following from *A House and its Head*:

> Nance Edgeworth was a tall, thin girl of twenty-four, with her father's head placed rather squarely on her shoulders, her mother's features set a little awry on her face, and an expression that was her own.

One feels that traits are sometimes added merely as means for exercising wit, as in the last clause of the description of the matron Miss James in *Two Worlds and Their Ways*:

> Her dark hair was arranged so plainly that it seemed to need a more negative word; her features seemed to be impregnated with her expression; her clothes were so suitable that no one saw them, and her figure so thin that the same thing might be said.

But they can also be brilliant; the best is the unusually long one of Miriam, in *Manservant and Maidservant*:

> Miriam remained transfixed for a moment, her habit when addressed by Bullivant. She was a stolid-looking girl of sixteen, on whom the plumpness incident to this age had fallen in excessive measure. She had a round, red face, large, startled eyes, round, red arms, a mouth that, as it was generally open, may also be described as round and red, and a nose that must be described in this manner. Mortimer had met her on the stairs and asked if she enjoyed her life, and had not suspected that her reply that she did not know, was a true one. She had no standard by which to form her judgement. Cook showed her no unkindness, and Bullivant was almost kind, though he would hardly have noticed if she had appeared with another face, and had no idea how much she would have liked to do this. Cook acted towards her as her conscience dictated, and Bullivant felt that she was female and was not George.

A minor, quite meaningless, but amusing convention is that many of the characters' names are those of literary figures. There are a

Chaucer, a Bunyan, a Donne; both a Shelley and a Keats; a Bacon, a Swift, a Lamb; a Miss Mitford and two Hallams; and others.

The physical descriptions which introduce characters a reader usually forgets; instead he forms, as if he were reading a play, his own image of the *dramatis personae*. I should think this is fairly common among novel-readers: one remembers Becky Sharp's green eyes, but what colour are Amelia Sedley's? Pale blue, probably. Miss Compton-Burnett compliments her reader's imaginative powers even more boldly, and one might add, more in consistency with her general literary economy, by omitting virtually all description of setting. The reason may be that, as is said in *Mother and Son* of the companion/housekeeper Miss Burke, "She had learned that the setting of human experience was no key to itself." However, in four novels—*Brothers and Sisters*, *Manservant and Maidservant*, *Two Worlds and Their Ways*, and *A God and his Gifts*—a few details are supplied. For example, the house of the Mertons in the last-named novel "was book-lined and not without grace, and seemed like a home from an old university moved to the country, which in its essence and life it was." Perhaps the best description, one that might serve for the central house in all the novels, is given by the tutor Gideon Doubleday to his mother in *Manservant and Maidservant*. It is the home of the Lamb family that Gideon is describing:

> "What kind of a house is it?" said Gertrude.
>
> "Good to look at, less good to live in. Large and light and chill, and furnished with few and stately things."

It is the right setting for the events. One wishes that the central house in *A Heritage and its History* had been pictured, if only in a sentence or two, because to be the master of this house—the "Heritage" of the title—is the lifelong passion of the hero of that novel, Simon Challoner.

Rarest of all, especially in the later novels, is any physical description of action longer than an adverb or a phrase. When it does appear, it can be so effective that one marvels the more that a writer of such gifts should subjugate them to her greater aim. It is often what the classical author does not do that makes us admire what he does. *A Family and a Fortune* has more "stage directions" than most of the novels, but the following short example, which movingly dramatizes the isolation of a daughter's grief, is from the early novel *Brothers and*

Sisters, and occurs at the time of the death of Christian Stace, whose wife is (the tyrant) Sophia and whose daughter is Dinah:

> She left him, giving her smile at the door, and entered Dinah's room without knocking, as was her habit. Sophia never knocked, if she could help it, in her own house. Dinah was sitting on a chair, near to nothing else in the room, and looked up blindly at her mother.

For compression and precision and irony and pathos, the three sentences are in their way remarkable.

Within the central house there is almost always a power figure like Sophia Stace—mother, father, aunt, grandmother, grandfather—and critics have agreed to call this figure the tyrant. His will is challenged, without much success, by his dependants. The first round of the battle may take place at the breakfast table, where more than half the novels open. The events proper may begin with an arrival, as stories always have; later in the events one or more members of the family may leave the household; they always return.

After breakfast, where the conversation is as sharp as if all had been sleepless, the rest of the day is spent in conversation, scarcely interrupted, indeed spurred on, by tea or dinner, death or other disaster. Members of the family go for frequent walks; sometimes they go to church; occasionally they read newspapers and books: but the last two diversions are infrequent, since they impede the talk. Many *sotto voce* remarks are made, directed against the tyrant, and the tyrant overhears them (as he is sometimes intended to), or pretends not to, or sharply questions the speaker whether or not he has overheard. There is a minor convention of mimicry, which, like the *sotto voce* remarks, is a kind of helpless revenge. The speech of the characters is rich in quotations, especially from the Bible and Shakespeare; there are numerous tags, such as any educated person would know, from Milton, Tennyson, Browning, and so on. Quotation is never recondite; though there are references to Greek tragedies, there are no quotations from them, nor any from Latin, French, or any but English literature. The servants' hall is loud with hymns, and when the Bible is not being quoted, a Biblical phraseology often prevails. So much for the general impression the dialogue gives; I will discuss its conventions more specifically in the following section of the present chapter.

In each novel a secret is revealed. The secret may concern incest or illegitimacy or an inheritance, but the revelation serves more to clarify or intensify the *status quo* than to alter it. In all but three of the novels the secret is contained in a lost or suppressed letter, will, or other document. It is often the tyrant that has suppressed it. In *Elders and Betters* the awkward and ambitious young woman Anna Donne destroys a will in favour of her aunt and uncle and preserves a will in her own favour. This secret is one of the few that is never revealed. In some of the novels what happens to the letter or letters is as hard to keep straight as it is in Schiller's *Don Carlos*, that drama remarkable for the amount of correspondence. In *Two Worlds and Their Ways* the place of the letter or will is taken by a pair of wildly itinerant ear-rings, to chart whose wanderings, and to summarize what their career reveals of the characteristics and relationships among their various possessors, would require an elaborate diagram, or Miss Compton-Burnett herself. (I have, however, made the effort in Chapter VI.) The neatest example of this convention is found in *The Mighty and Their Fall*, where Lavinia tries to prevent her father Ninian's remarriage by hiding a letter of acceptance from his intended, while Ninian in turn is guilty of an effort to destroy the will of his brother which had made Lavinia an heiress. Thus father and daughter's sins are parallel; they are both revealed; but it is Lavinia we wish to forgive, because her sin comes from love, while her father's comes from avarice.

It will already have been seen that the novels concern power. To what extent do they concern class, money, and love, those other concerns of earlier novelists?

Class is certainly not the concern of these novels that it was with the Victorians. The head of the household is of the gentry, sometimes a baronet, never higher; there is no mobility among classes, nor any mention of it. There is an accepted order of masters and servants. Among professions engaged in are those of physician, lawyer, clergyman. The clergymen are fools (the Reverend Dr. Chaucer in *Daughters and Sons*), tyrants (Henry Bentley in *Pastors and Masters*), or unbelievers (Oscar Jekyll in *A House and its Head*). There are many writers, both successful and *manqués*; *Daughters and Sons* and *A God and his Gifts* have the most, three apiece. Schoolmasters and schoolmistresses abound. In one novel, *Elders and Betters*, two sons are employed with the government, presumably the civil service. There are no other professions.

Money is nearly as important as power in the novels, and is frequently the same thing: the expression "Money is power" is used, in those words, several times in the novels. If we are not told the exact incomes of characters, as in the novels of Jane Austen, we are given enough information to judge their financial status fairly closely; and the amounts of inheritances are sometimes specifically set forth. The pursuit of money leads in a train of vices: jealousy, avarice, meanness, miserliness, lack of charity, the closed heart. Lies are told, wills are destroyed, and murders are committed, nor need retribution follow, as moral sentimentality has dictated so much oftener in novels than in life. It may follow, and it may not follow. Crime pays, and then again it doesn't pay; but usually it pays in these books where the possession of money, no matter how ill-gotten, results in power and prestige and the ego triumphant. So much less of the external world appears, in terms of its ordinary data, the trivia of naturalistic data which makes up the upholstery of the usual novel, that the emphasis on money gains by contrast. But then this is true of everything in Miss Compton-Burnett's novels—what is omitted emphasizes what isn't, and the result is their classical clarity.

Love is the love of kindred, those who are related by blood. Although there are examples of deep love between man and wife, such as Sir Roderick and Lady Shelley in *Two Worlds and Their Ways*, the characteristic attachment is the love between parent and child, brother and sister, brother and brother, sister and sister. The passion of Sophia Stace for her husband Christian in *Brothers and Sisters* is explained by the fact that they too are brother and sister, as is discovered years after their marriage. There is the figure of a loose woman, unique among the novels, in *Men and Wives*, the frivolous Camilla Christy, but the deepest love of Matthew Haslam, who wishes to marry Camilla, is reserved for his mother, who wishes to prevent this marriage. Matthew's murder of his mother is in a sense a protest against the dreadfully crippling force which family affection can become. The family tragically triumphs. There is no distinction made, as there is in the Christian if not the Aristotelian ethic, between love and sexuality; the one shades off into and can become the other: so that incest is the norm. Miss Compton-Burnett is at home in areas into which Freud made portentous sallies. The Victorian novelist may also have made the family his familiar province, but he is a mere tourist compared with Miss Compton-Burnett. It would seem almost inevitable in so self-absorbed a family as the one in the central household that incest would occur or be barely averted. The concept of sexuality on which the novels are predicated gives rise to such typical remarks as that of a character in *A House and its Head* to Grant Edgeworth:

> "You are fortunate, Grant," said Oscar. "You have come near to marrying your sister, the obvious woman for a man to marry."

Nor is there anything less Victorian—less publicly or professedly Victorian—than the topic of homosexuality, which appears and reappears throughout the novels, most pronouncedly in *More Women than Men* and *Two Worlds and Their Ways*, two of the three novels—the other is *Pastors and Masters*—the scenes of which are laid, in part, in boarding schools. In *More Men than Women*, Felix Bacon has been Jonathan Swift's lover for twenty-two years, but, during the course of the novel, Felix marries, and Jonathan has, before the events of the novel, fathered a son illegitimately: the sexual lines are not drawn distinctly or, apparently, permanently. In the same novel, Maria Rosetti has borne an illegitimate child but has a strong relationship with another schoolmistress, Theodora Luke. Elsewhere in the novels there are people with traits which would usually be considered homosexual, like Gregory Haslam, with his predilection for old women, etc., in *Men and Wives*. There are strong attachments between two men and two women where friendship merges into something different—if the two things are different. In *Elders and Betters* we are told that the relationship between Cook and the housemaid Ethel "borders on excess"; whether or not lesbian, it is very funny. Throughout the novels there is a kind of camp humour, as in *Brothers and Sisters*, when Edward Dryden pays a call on Sarah Wake and her brother Julian:

> "These columbines are wonderful, Sarah," said Edward. "Did you grow them?"
>
> "I grew them, and cut them, and put them in that pot," said Julian. "Every little womanly touch in this cottage is mine."

No moral issue is ever raised about any manner of sexual behaviour; homosexuality simply exists, and in these novels it often supplies comedy; it is neither smart nor tragic nor socially significant nor does it wear any other of the guises it has repetitively worn in what seems like a million modern novels.

What should be emphasized last in finishing this generalized picture of the eighteen novels is that no two are alike, as of course they could not be. Someone once wittily remarked, "What I like about them is that when you have read them *all*, you have read *one* of them." But, despite all the conventions which have been here outlined, the *données* and the schemata more rigorous than we are used to in other novelists, still there is wide variation within the form and shifts in the focus of attention, as the account in Chapter VI of the novels one by one will show. Are they more like one another than the plays of Plautus or Seneca, Corneille or Molière? And if one likes them, one likes them. One wishes there were one hundred and eighty.

II

DIALOGUE AND DICTION

The most striking convention of all in Miss Compton-Burnett's books—which are "something between a novel and a play"—is that they are written in dialogue; ninety per cent or more of the words are spoken by a character. V. S. Pritchett has seen this convention in historical terms:

> . . . The novel, in her hands, approaches the play or scenario. She has got back to the English novel's early contact with the artifice of the theatre—as he [Robert Liddell] and many critics have noted, she is Congrevian—her economy is theatrical, her dialogue essentially if too profusely so, the habit of her characters dramatic and not discursive or analytical. Important action—a sudden death, a murder, a comedy of proposals of marriage—is often reduced to stage direction. The crises are fierce and short; the comedy full of reversals of incident and repetitions on different levels. There is above all the strong element of her chorus. All this is of the theatre and her books lend themselves well to theatrical reading. These technical innovations have been important. They break with the standardised techniques of the naturalistic novel, which is none the less dead for being predominant. This extraordinary novelist writing about a limited, out-of-date, indeed extinct society in a very artificial fashion, has hit upon what seems to me the most hopeful direction for the stagnant art of the novel: the direction of drama and its idiom. That happens also to be the tendency of popular entertainment.[4]

To be technical, one would probably call the point of view of Miss Compton-Burnett's novels the external point of view—that is, we do not enter into the minds of the characters. In a novel written by the external method we see the characters and hear them, and we also learn of them by what the author has to say about them; but since this particular author has relatively little to say about her characters, and we are in fact generally hearing them to the exclusion of hearing *about* them, we could call her method, the dramatic method, a subdivision of the external point of view, foregoing much of the range of authorial analysis which the latter method can afford. The dramatic method is perhaps the most difficult technique by which an author can reveal character, because dialogue must bear all the weight, it must be individual and connotative and have sufficient passion or wit to engage us. Flaubert used the external method intermittently, when he judged that his material could thus be most effectively conveyed; among more modern writers the external method, with all the advantages it offers of enlisting the reader's close attention, his judgment, and, most important, his imagination, has flourished conspicuously in the works of Wyndham Lewis, remarkably so in the sustained bravura passages which begin *The Apes of God*. But that further refinement of the external method, where the novelist all but disappears and the characters speak as characters in a play, is unique with Miss Compton-Burnett. Inevitably, style is fused with content, and the insistent objectivity of Miss Compton-Burnett's vision has found its necessary vehicle in the dramatic method. Just as, in Dostoevsky, the most *engagé* of writers chose the internal method to reach the taproot of moral motivation.

The books are of course not pure drama. There is a limited amount of authorial comment. We read the stage directions that an audience would only see carried out. They tend to be compressed: "There was a knock at the door, and Helen came into the room." There are descriptions of characters and settings, as mentioned above. What little this author has to say about her characters—the amount has steadily decreased in each novel from *Pastors and Masters* to *A God and his Gifts*—occasionally takes the form of an amusing comment, either on the person speaking or on people in general:

> "I wish it was us who had a party," said Tilly, who was an almost startling example of failure to rise above a lack of advantages. (*Brothers and Sisters*)

> "I must try to conquer myself," said his wife, with the sigh natural to this purpose. (*Parents and Children*)

It is very rare in these books that we see a person thinking. When we do, it strikes us as odd, alien to the dramatic texture; note the exclamation points in the following passage from an early work, *Brothers and Sisters*, which seem like an attempt to inject drama into the consciousness of a character:

> The funeral party was shown into Christian's study, where the will was to be read. Sophia had found it fitting that her husband's will should be read from her husband's place. It seemed to her that in his own room it would be his own voice speaking! People who grieved but gently for him, should take the benefits coming from his death from his own hands. Of his own will he should give them, not forced by his death, not by giving up all himself! Thus Sophia dealt with the surge within her.

It is one of the few awkward passages in the novels. For one or two other examples of the internal method:

> Josephine looked from him to Helen, as if she hardly followed his words. Afterwards she seemed to remember hearing her own voice, coming after a crash and through the ensuing din. (*More Women than Men*)

> Venice fixed her eyes in front of her, while a great pleasure welled up within her. (*Parents and Children*)

The effect is strangely disturbing to the reader's involvement, the opposite effect of the internal method in the customary novel. Ordinarily a character's thoughts are guessed by what he says or by what we might judge them to be: "as if" and "seems" constructions, at least in the early novels, are therefore frequent:

> "Now how can I help you?" said Josephine, in an open, considering tone, as if the foregoing talk had left little impression on her mind.

The dramatic method allows an unusual ease and economy of transition from scene to scene. Felix Bacon, another character in *More Women than Men*, finishes one conversation, and, in the following sentence, is miles away at his father's house:

> A few hours later Felix was greeting Sir Robert Bacon. "Well, Felix, you have come to see me die?"

Such speed of transition can be disconcerting, but once one is used to it, which does not take long, it can make other more artful transitional devices seem a little portentous—for example, the connective stratagem used by Virginia Woolf in *Mrs. Dalloway*, the chiming of Big Ben, which is heard by different people in different places. Miss Compton-Burnett is like Shakespeare, arbitrary and sudden: "Another part of the forest."

One might expect that the author would avail herself of another means used in the drama proper of presenting a character's thoughts—the soliloquy: a device used from Aeschylus to Tennessee Williams. But I have noted only three soliloquies in the novels (one each in *Men and Wives, A Family and a Fortune*, and *The Mighty and Their Fall*). Perhaps it is only their rarity that makes them seem to ring false.

Mr. Robert Liddell has listed about two hundred and fifty ways in which the characters may speak, from " 'consideringly, cordially, drily, earnestly, easily,' " etc., to a note of the " 'scolding, piercing, unsparing, wary, wistful.' "[5] Nonetheless, for every adverb or adjective of "stage direction," there are ten times when the manner of a character's speaking is not described—when there is merely "he said" or "she said" or nothing at all. Mr. Liddell was analysing those novels published by 1955; in the four novels published since then the gradual elimination of these adjectives and adverbs has accelerated. The dialogue speaks for itself so exactly that the author need not help the reader to hear the tone of voice.

What, then, does the dialogue sound like? Its chief characteristic is its terseness. It is stylized; if a sentence is short, and it usually is, it is a simple subject-verb declarative sentence; if it is longer, it is often two compound clauses which employ parallelism or antithesis. Thus it has an unusual balance and symmetry. The tendency to rhetorical exactitude recalls Corneille.

The dialogue is most exact and lucid. The characters never speak ungrammatically or in dialect, never interrupt one another or lose the thread, never grope for expression or struggle to capture the half-formed thought: they mean what they say, and they say what they mean, and they say it all of the time. The dialogue is like Shaw's, where the people answer one another with a military regularity; it is not like Chekhov's, where they frequently do not. Since remark builds upon remark, the dialogues progress—again like Shaw, again unlike Chekhov. Frank Kermode has said that the dialogue moves forward "by exploiting in each remark unobvious logical and syntactical implications in the previous one."[6] Here is the beginning of *Manservant and Maidservant*:

> "Is that fire smoking?" said Horace Lamb.
>
> "Yes, it appears to be, my dear boy."

"I am not asking what it appears to be doing. I asked if it was smoking."

"Appearances are not held to be a clue to the truth," said his cousin. "But we seem to have no other."

Horace advanced into the room as though his attention were withdrawn from his surroundings.

"Good morning," he said in a preoccupied tone, that changed as his eyes resumed their direction. "It does seem that the fire is smoking."

"It is in the stage when smoke is produced. So it is hard to see what it can do."

"Do you really not understand me?"

"Yes, yes, my dear boy. It is giving out some smoke. We must say that it is."

The dialogue can give the impression of fairly bristling with syntax; one seems to hear a rattling of the bones of grammar. Elizabeth Bowen, writing in 1941, said that "to read in these days a page of Compton-Burnett dialogue is to think of the sound of glass being swept up, one of these London mornings after a blitz."[7]

The wit of the dialogue—probably the chief reason the novels are read—comes, especially in the later novels, from the persistent use of irony and of ironic paradox. The later novels rely much less on the comedy of character where the funniness of a remark depends to a degree on the fact that a certain person is saying it; the comedy becomes more intellectual. To take a character at random here is Ursula Scrope, one of the most intelligent people in *The Present and the Past* (1953), and three of her remarks chosen at random from a brief scene in that novel:

"We think other people forget themselves because they pretend to, and we assume they think it of us in the same way. There is one thing to be said for not surviving after death. We shall not know them when they know our hearts, and when we know theirs. The second would be the worst."

"Perhaps that is the difference between a bad person and a good; that the one reveals himself, and the other has the proper feeling to hide it."

"I cannot bear people who try to be brave . . . There is the danger that they may succeed, and it is even worse than other kinds of success."

A reviewer of *The Mighty and Their Fall* wrote in *The Times Literary Supplement* that "In the dialogue as a whole drama is now and then sacrificed to sententiousness."[8] Is "sententious" the right word? How is "sacrifice" involved? The play of gnomic wit, of axiom, paradox, exploded cliché, is in the late novels like a glittering dance. I do not think Ursula Scrope would be out of place in the *Oresteia*, where Agamemnon says (two thousand years before La Rochefoucauld), "There are few whose inborn love / Warms without envy to a friend's prosperity," and where, when the Chorus praises Cassandra: "Courage and destiny in you / Are proudly matched," Cassandra answers, "The happy never hear such praise."[9] This grim succinctness is one of the qualities that allies Miss Compton-Burnett most closely to the tragedians, although it is certainly true that Ursula has more of a sense of humour than Cassandra.

The truth-speaking people in the novels like Ursula examine clichés to explode them; the people less than sincere reveal their insincerity by their reliance on clichés. An extreme example is Cassius Clare in the same novel, whose metaphors are trite to the extent of, "So I took the bull by the horns and walked up to the cannon's mouth." A special type of comic cliché, pompous, Biblical and grand, is heard in the servants' hall, where butlers like Bullivant in *Manservant and Maidservant* and Ainger in *The Present and the Past* lord it over their subordinates, or attempt to.

There is a quality of abstractness to the dialogue, particularly in the use of indefinite pronouns, which some of the above examples will show. It is markedly unsensuous. Which, indeed, can be said of the general texture of the novels: Evelyn Waugh has written, "She is the least sensuous of writers. There is no flavour of food or wine, no scene-painting of landscape or architecture, no costume, no visual image even of the characters; ages are stated; height, bulk, strength or infirmity gently suggested; sometimes a moustache or a beard is mentioned, but there is never anything approaching a portrait."[10]

There is another kind of language reserved for scenes of high emotion. Here the wit disappears and a strident and theatrical asseveration takes over. The following comes from a climactic moment in *Manservant and Maidservant*; Charlotte Lamb is speaking to her husband, the apparently reformed tyrant Horace, about her elopement with his cousin Mortimer:

> "I shall speak of it to you," said Charlotte on the instant. "We will not have a great and unnatural silence. Mortimer and I could not suffer the things in this house; we were at the end of our power to suffer. We could let helpless children suffer no longer, after seeing them do so all their lives. We thought of the way of escape for us all, and we were going to take it.

It would have been the right way, and the only right one. But I have come home to find this difference, this difference that there might always have been. If you had been like this always, Horace! If you had lived this life from the first! This is proof that you could have done so, that you could have made the hard path easy. It does not show the past years in a better light. But for the moment our case is gone. Whether it may return or not, is another thing, but for the moment it is gone. The future is in your hands, and you have the power to hold it. But the past is my tragedy and your fault. You must not be a martyr. You put me to a longer martyrdom."

These passages, which are rare, have a certain appeal; they once again recall, if anything, the bombast of Corneille. But Corneille is consistent, and such speeches as Charlotte's just given are odd, even jarring contrasts with the general texture of wit. Angus Wilson, in comparing Miss Compton-Burnett with Wilde, has said, "There is . . . something strangely akin in their combination of the language and wit of high comedy with the plots of melodrama. She does not, of course, lapse so easily into the language of melodrama as Wilde, but there are purple passages in her work which are by no means intended ironically."[11]

A much more common, and it seems to me much less discerning, criticism of the dialogue is that it is unnatural. It is often said that people simply don't talk the way Compton-Burnett people talk. The answer is of course that people never talk the way people in novels talk. Here is Shirley, the heroine of Charlotte Brontë's novel, describing her problems with the cook:

"I have lectured her on the duty of being careful . . . in a way quite new to her. So eloquent was I on the text of economy that I surprised myself; for, you see, it is altogether a fresh idea. I never thought, much less spoke, on the subject till lately. But it is all theory; for when I came to the practical part I could retrench nothing. I had not firmness to take off a single pound of butter, or to prosecute to any clear result an inquest into the destiny of either dripping, lard, bread, cold meat, or other kitchen perquisite whatever. I know we never get up illuminations at Fieldhead, but I could not ask the meaning of sundry quite unaccountable pounds of candles. We do not wash for the parish, yet I viewed in silence items of soap and bleaching-powder calculated to satisfy the solicitude of the most anxious inquirer after our position in reference to those articles. Carnivorous I am not, nor is Mrs. Pryor, nor is Mrs. Gill herself, yet I only hemmed and opened my eyes a little wide when I saw butchers' bills whose figures seemed to prove that fact—falsehood, I mean. Caroline, you may laugh at me, but you can't change me. I am a poltroon on certain points; I feel it. There is a base alloy of moral cowardice in my composition. I blushed and hung my head before Mrs. Gill, when she ought to have been faltering confessions to me. I found it impossible to get up the spirit even to hint, much less to prove, to her that she was a cheat. I have no calm dignity, no true courage about me."

What the objection to the unnaturalness of Miss Compton-Burnett's dialogue amounts to is, once again, the fact that we are used to another convention of dialogue, we are used to the diction of Dickens or the naturalistic diction—itself highly formalized—of some modern novels. Miss Compton-Burnett has simply adopted a different convention. Kingsley Amis is saying more about himself than about Miss Compton-Burnett when he objects to the restrictions of her dialogue:

> What is striking is less what the characters say than the remarkable number of kinds of thing they do not say. To imagine what would have to happen before a Compton-Burnett character could say "You bore me" or "What a pretty dress" or "Give me a kiss" or "Oh my God" is an instructive experience. The majority of these conversations are marathon tennis-matches in which the ball always lands in court. Any given return may be a smash, a screw-shot or a plain lob to the base-line—very occasionally it may come off the wood—but no ball ever rebounds from a player's head instead of his racquet, or gets angrily kicked into the net, or is chucked over the wire into the cabbage-patch.[12]

What this tells us, outside the fact that Mr. Amis plays tennis, is that Mr. Amis refuses to accept a certain convention of dialogue different from his own. One doesn't hear "What a pretty dress" in Racine or Dostoevsky. And it tells us how naturalistic Mr. Amis' novels are, if we had any doubts.

Miss Compton-Burnett has told me that to her the characters in her novels speak differently one from another, but even Edward Sackville-West, who has written discerningly of her work, has said, ". . . Everyone in these novels employs the same tone and the same large and scholarly vocabulary."[13] On the contrary, the range of tone within its stylized limits is remarkable, and the vocabulary is by no means large: it is much closer to the two thousand words of Racine than the thirty thousand of Shakespeare. I would agree with Henry Reed who has said that ". . . despite the conventionalised tone in which almost all her characters speak, no other living writer can manage so clearly to distinguish between the various members of a large cast—sometimes approaching twenty in number."[14] And when her characters are gathered in a large group, she manages them well; everyone speaks often enough, and naturally enough, that we know everyone is there.

One can give endless examples of how people talk like themselves. In *Manservant and Maidservant*, for example, George talks like a workhouse boy, Miriam is genuinely naïve, Miss Buchanan is the epitome of the terse, Avery is childlike, Bullivant is fond of the big platitude. People have speech habits: there are Edgar's hesitations in *A Family and a Fortune*, Dulcia's exclamations in *A House and its Head*, Spong's oily tritenesses in *Men and Wives*, little Henry's "Oh, dear, oh, dear!" in *The Present and the Past*, or Catherine's "short, quick sentences" in the same novel. People ride conversational hobby-horses; how often Jane Seymour in *Daughters and Sons* talks of her "two great men," her brother and nephew; how often Rachel Hardisty in *Men and Wives* speaks of death; and there are the misty pieties of Beatrice Fellowes in *A House and its Head*. If at first two characters seem to speak alike, closer attention will show they are not the same; for example, two women with an obvious genius for the laconic are Mrs. Frost, a cook in *The Present and the Past*, and the superb Miss Munday in *More Women than Men*. But they are quite different: Miss Munday is more droll than Mrs. Frost, and quite willing to make a joke of herself; Mrs. Frost's tone is harder, less self-amused, but with an equal appetite for the absurd. Here is Josephine Napier, owner of the girls' school in *More Women than Men*, in conversation with two of the mistresses in the school, Miss Rosetti and Miss Munday:

> "Experience is not a matter of doors and walls," said Josephine, glancing round. "Though other things may be a matter of them sometimes."
>
> "The deepest experience always takes place within them," said Miss Rosetti.
>
> "Yes, yes, indeed," said Josephine. "That is profound."
>
> "I have a great deal of knowledge of life," said Miss Munday.
>
> "If I may say so, I have noticed it," said Josephine. "And again if I may say so, I have noticed it increasing."
>
> "You may say so again," said Miss Munday.

Here is a brief example of Mrs. Frost in the servants' hall; Ainger, the butler, has just been given a cigar by the master. Halliday is the general man:

"In all the years I have been in this house," said Halliday, "I have never had a cigar offered me."

"Neither have I," said Mrs. Frost.

One defect that could be said to exist in the dialogue arises directly from its obvious virtue of intellectual energy. And it is related to what we have noted of the lack of sense data in the novels. The dialogue occasionally takes on a kind of dry, febrile, attenuated quality; a point is pursued into nothingness and beyond; the coach clatters on down the cobblestones, but the occupants have disappeared. The wit can become pert, a little snippy; their sniping at one another can come to seem unrealistically, heartlessly protracted. Occasionally the paradoxes don't work; in *Darkness and Day*, for example, someone says, "You are too weak to face your weakness, and there is no truer strength": true in a sense, but that sense is so much less apparent than the plain lack of logic. But for one time that the dialogue fails in any of these respects, it succeeds a hundred times, it sustains itself page after easy page in happy brilliancy.

The dialogue is perhaps as near pure prose as writing can be. There is not an ounce of poetry in it. This is no objection, because the aim was prose. The aim was not beauty, and yet a rare beauty does arise, as in the following scene from *Parents and Children*. It is the scene of the return of Fulbert, who has been presumed dead, to his family; Regan is his very old mother, and Nevill his very young son:

> Nevill ran into the room and towards his grandmother, caught sight of his father, paused and rested his eyes on him, and then ran on and laid something on Regan's lap.
>
> "A bird's nest," he said. "Where the little birds used to live."
>
> "What will they do without their home?"
>
> "All fly away," said Nevill.
>
> "The little birds had a father and mother bird," said Regan, guiding his head towards Fulbert. "And the father bird has come back to the nest."
>
> Nevill cast his eyes about in quest of this visitor, and dropped them to the nest, in case Regan's words might be true.
>
> "Where?" he said, bringing them back to her face.
>
> "Look and see," said Regan, turning his head again in the right direction.
>
> "Outside," said Nevill, as some sparrows chirped by the window. "He has come back. Hark."

The diction of Miss Compton-Burnett's novels, in its intelligence, compression, and precision, demands the close attention of the reader. She must be read either carefully or not at all. With her readers, those modern readers who have not been totally dulled and deadened by a language overused, worn smooth, she succeeds in commanding a full attention. Though in how different a way, the effect has been the same as that of the style of Henry James in his late novels, whose convolutions are freighted with rich intimations, or of the mature style of James Joyce, which destroyed one language and nearly succeeded in creating another. Surely the primary technical problem of the modern novelist has been to find a diction, to make himself uniquely heard in the clamorous stale tide of words. That she has found a diction as if by instinct, when Joyce's or James' career amounts to the entirely conscious pursuit of one, is no less to her great credit.

III

STRUCTURE: THE TRIPLE PATTERN

The action that punctuates the flow of words in Miss Compton-Burnett's novels may be violent, sudden, and melodramatic, but it occurs offstage. Most of the novels contain at least one death; in *Brothers and Sisters* there are four. Action serves primarily as an incentive to conversation, and can give the impression of arbitrary and imposed, rather than organic, event. Kingsley Amis has said of the lack of diversity of incident and its function which he finds in Miss Compton-Burnett's novels, ". . . The real objection to the author's method is not that her books are held together by melodramatic, or improbable, or reduplicated events, but that they are not so held together."[15] To meet this objection, one can say, first of all, that some of the plots, such as those of *Two Worlds and Their Ways* and *Mother and Son*, proceed very naturally and cohesively, event growing out of event smoothly, necessarily.

Moreover, though plot may be the most elementary, even primitive, of our interests in fiction, it is no more than that. As Ortega has said in his "Notes on the Novel," "The action or plot is not the substance of a novel but its scaffolding, its mechanical prop. The essence of the novel—that is to say, of the modern novel—does not lie in 'what happens' but precisely in the opposite: in the personages' pure living, in their being and being thus, above all, in the ensuing milieu."[16] Action in a novel, Ortega says, is "a mere pretext—the string, as it were, that makes the beads into a necklace."[17] Either I misinterpret Mr. Amis or judge too much by his own practice but it would seem that he would want the string more visible, more obviously functional. I do not see why it should be. Also, to Mr. Amis' objection one could answer with James' famous sentence in "The Art of Fiction," "We must grant the artist his subject, his idea, his *donnée*: our criticism is applied only to what he makes of it." It is "the personages' pure living" with which Miss Compton-Burnett is concerned and which we as readers are asked to observe.

As for the improbabilities, think of what reckless imposition of unlikelihoods one must grant Shakespeare. And, on the other hand, is it not lifelike for events to occur arbitrarily and suddenly? Life is seldom enough like the ideal recipe for a novel offered by some literary theorists where plot grows out of character and character grows out of plot. Life does not run on such rails. Simply, it is more surprising, and it is very improbable. Miss Compton-Burnett's surprises are, it is true, not the kind which most of us meet with in our lives. But to reject them as insufficiently worked into the total fabric of the novel is really only to say that we are habituated to another kind of novel, an elder convention of realism and romance, which, despite its survival in certain modern highly gifted authors like Mr. Amis, is now outworn. Miss Compton-Burnett has said, grimly enough, "As regards plots I find real life no help at all. Real life seems to have no plots, and as I think a plot desirable and almost necessary, I have this extra grudge against life."[18] In any case the novels are not organized by their "melodramatic, or improbable, or reduplicated events," but by the themes their titles suggest. The themes erupt, as it were, into events. Finally, "The sad, false chapter is over," and nothing much has changed.

If the plots seem unlikely and sometimes even absurd when summarized, so do most plots. *King Oedipus* has an absurd plot; so does *La Vida Es Sueño*. I should say that absurdity is a necessary element of all our fictions; in a sense it is what fiction is.

Why should there be a plot at all? Miss Compton-Burnett has said that "a plot has to be imposed . . . because a book must have form."[19] In her novels the conventions of plot do not obscure, indeed they even support, the greater realities—that things do not much change, that the dead are not missed, that people become their guises, that evil may or may not be punished. There must be form because form liberates: it frees, it enhances, it is the catalyst. Why is it that plot is so much frailer in the literary novel of our century? It could be that the disappearance, at least the submersion, of plot is related to the disappearance of order in nonfictional life. A belief in social hierarchy; a public morality; institutions, like marriage, which were not questioned as institutions: these allowed plot, which was an echo of the external order that the artist perceived. Joyce supplies plot in *Ulysses* by the superimposition of Greek myth; Miss Compton-Burnett by the clanging machinery of melodrama. But how often what there is of plot in the modern novel is servantlike and simple—in Firbank or Virginia Woolf plot is much less closely related to meaning than it is in Thackeray or Jane Austen.

In Chapter VI where the novels are discussed one by one their structure is individually dealt with, but in summarizing the conventions of structure here one can point out various recurrent features. It has already been mentioned that in most of the novels people go away and return, drawn back unresisting to the maelstrom of family life. There are variations; Rosebery, in *Mother and Son*, pretends that he is going away—Rosebery is full of pretences—but doesn't. Sometimes departures are voluntary, and sometimes not; for example, Harriet Haslam in *Men and Wives* is taken to an asylum for the insane. The two most striking kinds of events in all the novels are deaths and revelations. Most of the novels begin with an arrival, or somewhere later in the story a person new to the scene appears, either arrival affecting the composition of forces in the scene.

One notices over and over a triple pattern, an arrangement of event and motif and revelation in rhythmic and inevitable threesome. From the three governesses in *Daughters and Sons* to the triple marriage with which *Elders and Betters* ends, a tendency to the use of threes is everywhere. In *More Women than Men* Josephine loses the three men in her life—Simon, Gabriel, and Felix; in *A House and its Head*, Duncan has three successive wives—Ellen, Alison, and Cassie; in *Manservant and Maidservant* Horace Lamb is three times brought close to death. In *Two Worlds and Their Ways*, which seems the most consciously structured of the eighteen, there are three principal exposures of "cheating"—Clemence at her school, her brother Sefton at his, and then their parents' more adult misdeeds, this basic pattern reinforced by a host of peripheral revelations of misconduct among other members of the household. I do not think that most readers notice the triple structure any more consciously than they hear, when listening to a Mozart sonata, the exposition, development, and recapitulation. But it is there, and it is harmonious. There is the sense of a cycle, of the wheel coming round: in the process of which revolution, much has been exposed.

IV

THE USE OF CONVENTIONS

Dr. Stockmann, Ibsen's "Enemy of the People," says that "truths are not such tough old Methuselahs as most people imagine. A normal, ordinary truth is good for, say, seventeen or eighteen—at most twenty years; seldom more. And truths as venerable as that are nothing but skin and bones; yet it isn't until then that the great majority adopts them and prescribes them to Society as wholesome spiritual food. But there's not much nourishment in that kind of a diet, I assure you . . ."[20]

Those conventions of Miss Compton-Burnett's novels described in the present chapter—without, I hope, sounding too much like an I.B.M. machine—are, of course, literary conventions: customs, usages, proprieties, the commitments faithfully observed of a scrupulous literary sense. They have the brilliant appeal of the formal, the elegant, and the assured. There is another sense of the word "convention," especially evident in its adjective "conventional," which refers to social usages and customs—the way in which people follow patterns in their daily lives and observe some kind of code of social behaviour, whether it is in taking their meals at regular hours or in any other way conforming to the habits of well-bred society. Miss Compton-Burnett's characters are, in social terms, very conventional; given their period, their class, and their intelligence, it would be highly improbable if they were not. They never throw bricks; the varieties of behaviour in which they do *not* engage seem severely limited to readers used to the belches and the bowels of the naturalistic novel. That life is more various than any naturalistic novel would now seem to have been the inevitable defeat of the aim of naturalism; inevitably, even in *Ulysses*, the flux of experience, which is life, must be dealt with selectively and reduced into some formal pattern, which is the novel. Some of Miss Compton-Burnett's most intelligent characters are eloquent in their support of the social convention. "And convention is usually so sound that it is right to be a slave to it," says Ursula Scrope in *The Present and the Past*, and, in the same novel, Flavia Clare says, "It is a mistake to ignore conventions. There is always a reason behind them."

But perhaps we can be permitted to distinguish still a third type of convention, and that is the convention of the received notion, the truth so dated that it is no longer true, of which Dr. Stockmann speaks. I do not mean that the novels advocate an unconventional morality; they advocate nothing: but I would suggest that beneath all the literary conventions, in the midst of the social conventions which the characters are observing, there is a revolutionary anti-conventional spirit working. It is very modern. It may take a violent form in the actions of some characters, that of violent protest against the social proprieties; the civilized may suddenly revert to the natural primitive and produce murder or those other acts of extreme anti-social nature of which the plots are full. This, indeed, may be the final explanation of what seems to be that vast disparity between order and sudden outrage which the novels so surprisingly manifest. They are the two sides of the coin. The order is the polished talk; the outrage is both its end and its opposite. At one point in *A Family and a Fortune* we are told that "The present seemed a surface scene, acted over a seething life, which had been calmed but never dead."

But I think that there is a related but positive revolutionary spirit, most intimately conveyed in the talk itself. If one examines the texture of the conversation closely, particularly the words of the most intelligent people in the novels, one will see that at its sharpest it largely consists of a puncturing of platitudes of all kinds—moral, social, psychological. They are examined, and rejected, in a series of small deft explosions. The following passage from *Darkness and Day* is typical. The speakers are Sir Ransom Chace, a man of eighty-eight; Anne and Emma, his spinster daughters; and Gaunt Lovat, his friend:

> "I suppose in effect you two live for your father?" said Gaunt to the sisters.
>
> "We hope it is the effect," said Anne.
>
> "So do I," said Sir Ransom. "It gives me a better position in the scheme of things. I have enough pity."
>
> "I never see why people should have it for being old," said Gaunt.
>
> "Everyone else does. You want some reason for not giving it."
>
> "We are supposed to like to pity people."
>
> "We only like to look down on them for needing pity."

"Well, why should I not do that?"

"You are too attached to me. It would have to be real pity, and people do not like that. They are not equal to it."

"Old people have their share of the past, if not of the future."

"Well, there is the matter in a word," said Sir Ransom. "People only count the future. They do not really live in the past. They have forgotten it."

"You cannot eat your cake and have it."

"That is a mean saying. You could, if you had enough cake. It is sad that it has become established. It throws a dark light on human nature."

Sir Ransom Chace is one of the truth-seekers and truth-speakers in the novels. There are several dozen like him, no two quite alike, from Emily Herrick in *Pastors and Masters* to Joanna Egerton in *A God and his Gifts*. With smiling irony and buoyant cynicism they pierce to the core of the cliché; their weapon is paradox. They are among the most attractive people Miss Compton-Burnett has created, or that anyone has created; wry, self-mocking, entirely honest; amusing, civilized, and profound. Within the rigidity of the literary framework that bounds them, their elasticity is unlimited; so firm a discipline or form allows their range, their freedom and their humanity.

CHAPTER THREE

SECRETS

> "Civilised life exacts its toll. We live among the civilised."
> "The conventions are on the surface," said his wife. "We know the natural life is underneath."
> "We do; we have our reason. But we cannot live it. We know the consequences of doing so. If not, we learn."
>
> —*A Heritage and its History*

The uneasy truce between the natural instinct and the social instinct, between the "natural life" and the codes of social convention, between, in Freudian terms, the id and the superego, gives much of the conversation in Miss Compton-Burnett's novels a feeling of perilous poise. It is as if her people were standing with their backs to an abyss, aware that it is there, while they talk on, shedding their own light, more dazzling from its contrast with the black gulf on whose rim they are poised. Sometimes they stop talking, and we see only the abyss. At these moments a secret is revealed.

The central theme of the novels can be regarded as the search for truth. We have mentioned those bright ironic people whose constant habit is the mocking of the tired and trite conventional falsity. On their deep level they serve to tell us what is true; it is often enough not the surface level on which things are true. Beneath the necessary decorums of a regulated and orderly life are the dark springs of conduct which cannot finally be repressed. If we decide that this is too negative a view of human nature, one which neglects the forces for kindness and love and generosity that there must be in human nature since we see, or think we see, the evident signs of them, it may be that we reject it emotionally rather than intellectually and simply find it too hard, too Greek and too comfortless. And it is true that we might reject the home truths which the novels contain as too grim, in literary terms alone, if it were not for the wit which rescues all.

The novels are full of references to the life beneath the conventions, and these references are in themselves steps in the search for truth. The less than perfectly intelligent people sometimes make the mistake of taking the surface for the substance:

> "What is all this mystery?" said Maria, in an exasperated manner. "Why should not school be an open and natural life, like any other?"
>
> "Like what other?" said Mr. Firebrace. (*Two Worlds and Their Ways*)

Or of denying the darkness of the subsurface truths:

> "Ah, to know all is to forgive all," said Rhoda.
>
> "I confess I have not found it so, my lady" [says the butler Deakin]. "To forgive, it is best to know as little as possible." (*A Heritage and its History*)

Here are some of the young Mowbray cousins in *A Father and his Fate*:

> "You talk as if you had something to hide."
>
> "As if I had many things to hide, as we all should talk."
>
> "I do not think I have more than is inevitable."
>
> "I daresay I have not either."
>
> "He is sure he has not," said Nigel. "He has been trained in self-esteem."
>
> "I think I have," said Ursula.
>
> "I am sure I have," said Audrey.
>
> "I only hope I hide them," said Rudolf.
>
> "I trust I am not a transparent person," said Nigel.
>
> "I can say that I should not mind, if Mother looked into my heart at this moment," said Constance.
>
> "Think again," said Malcolm. "And imagine her really doing so."
>
> There was a pause.

It was a particularly conventional society that Miss Compton-Burnett has set the time of her novels in. In class and milieu, in long Victorian tradition, this society had grown so rigid that departures from its codes appear by contrast particularly violent. Miss Compton-Burnett herself has said of the inhabitants of her chosen milieu, "They were highly moral people. Therefore they took great pains to conceal their wrong-doings."[1] But since it is also a transitional period, as the rigidity itself shows, the violent outbreaks of instinct can appear premonitory, an historical index of the unease with which conventions were being maintained. Rather than the conscious employment of the historical sense, however, it is probably merely a normal instance of an artist's sensitivity to his environment, particularly that of his early years.

A secret is born when temptation arises, is succumbed to, and the results concealed. In the most frequently quoted remark in her conversation with Margaret Jourdain in *Orion* in 1945, Miss Compton-Burnett said, ". . . I think there are signs that strange things happen, though they do not emerge. I believe it would go ill with many of us, if we were faced by a strong temptation, and I suspect that with some of us it does go ill."[2] It is an intelligent and moral woman, Teresa Chilton in *The Mighty and Their Fall*, who says, "We all have it in us to do those things. There have been times when I might have done them, if I had dared." It is generally, but not invariably, the people in a position of power who succumb.

Ellen Mowbray, in *A Father and his Fate*, says that "a real secret is a rare thing." Over and over in the novels the secret—and it never is an agreeable surprise—is revealed. Most of us would probably agree that secrets are hard to keep, and that they are seldom kept; but the insistence with which secrets are pursued and uncovered in these novels is intimidating. It is excusable, however, in thematic terms: it is a sign that the truth is what is being sought for, that the truth will out, that the truth is supremely important. That the truth will make us free, is another matter. It is one of the legends that have grown up about the fad of psychoanalysis that if we know the true origin of our emotional disturbances, they will, most magically, evanesce. The fact is, that to stand in the hard clear light of truth does not of itself make us any happier. It can often (as it does in Ibsen's plays) make us quite a bit unhappier. There are other values besides happiness, of course. The search for truth is a Greek occupation; it is one of the Greek aspects of a Compton-Burnett novel. At the end of one of them it is not that the *status quo* is altered: it is that we know what the *status quo* is.

There is great variety and interest in the secrets motif in the novels, and to examine them one by one from this standpoint will show the structural importance of the motif. In *Pastors and Masters*, the first of the eighteen, the secret of the authorship of the manuscript supplies the frail plot. That it is neither the original work of Nicholas Herrick nor the recently written work of Richard Bumpus becomes known to two people, Nicholas's sister Emily and her friend Theresa Fletcher, but the knowledge spreads no further. It serves to corroborate the intellectual shoddiness of Nicholas, but does not alter Emily's love for him, and in fact induces an ironic admiration.

The whole process of *Brothers and Sisters* is the double revelation—first, that Mrs. Lang is Christian Stace's mother, and second, that

Christian Stace and his wife Sophia had had the same father—that is, that they are half-brother and sister. An effort, quite unsuccessful, is made to keep the latter a secret. The revelations serve to isolate the Stace children, Andrew, Dinah, and Robin, until finally, at the end of the novel, they stand alone in bleak recognition of their solitude.

The rapidity with which secrets are uncovered is especially shown in *Men and Wives*, where, within a few minutes after Matthew Haslam has told Camilla Christy that he has murdered his mother, Camilla, with that febrile loquacity which is typical of her, has informed two other people. Matthew's motives for murdering his mother are complex, one of them being the excess of his love for her. The immediate reason, however, is that he thinks she will prevent his marriage to Camilla, and one of the resultant ironies is that when Camilla learns of the murder, she refuses to marry him.

In *More Women than Men* the repressive atmosphere of a girls' school is the appropriate milieu for the hiding of truths and their curious disclosure. The truth of Gabriel Swift's parentage, that he is the illegitimate son of Maria Rosetti, comes out, but the murder of his wife Ruth by the aunt who adores him—Josephine, the tyrant of the novel—becomes known only to Maria. Josephine offers Maria a partnership in her school as "hush money," and the novel ends, oddly enough, in the firm quasi-lesbian bond between the two women, founded on secrets as much as on their natural propensities.

In *A House and its Head*, Grant Edgeworth seduces his uncle Duncan's second wife Alison. Duncan is the tyrant of the novel, and the grand stern contempt in his treatment of his nephew, when the truth of the child's parentage is revealed, is typical of the blind pride of the tyrant. It is interesting to trace in this novel how gradually the truth of the parentage of the baby comes out; step by step one can follow the truth struggling for the light, aided by the prurient curiosity of other families in the village. The murder of the baby which Grant's wife Sibyl, daughter to Duncan, arranges, is cloaked by the repressive horror of the crime, and becomes known only to her husband, her sister, and her stepmother.

In *Daughters and Sons*, it is a tyrant *manqué*, Hetta Ponsonby, who reveals the central mystery of the two anonymous gifts of £1,000 to her brother, the hard-pressed writer John Ponsonby. The gifts, she informs him, have come from his daughter France, who has, unknown to him, become a successful writer herself and who has kept her literary career a secret from her father because, as much as she loves him, she fears his jealousy. If Hetta had been established firmly in a position of power, the secret would probably not have been revealed; it is typical of the tyrants that they repress the truth lest it make their dependants independent in thought and judgment.

The one secret in *A Family and its Fortune* is not an important one, nor is it very convincing. Clement Gaveston, having received some money from his uncle Dudley's inheritance, becomes a miser; the discovery of this fact is regarded with rather more reprobation by his family than by the reader. Clement's hoarding of the money supports the central theme, of the corrupting force of avarice, but it is a minor incident oddly placed in a climactic position, and in fact the ending events of this novel are curiously weak. The illumination of some larger or darker or more reverbatory mystery might, one is tempted to speculate, have organized this novel better.

In *Parents and Children*, Fulbert Sullivan has gone away on a long voyage and has been presumed dead. His wife Eleanor is wooed and won by a neighbour, Ridley Cranmer. Fulbert returns to England, though not to his home, and writes to Ridley; but Ridley, intent on his approaching marriage (and on his becoming stepfather to Eleanor and Fulbert's nine children!), conceals the letter. In a fine scene the disloyalty and duplicity of Ridley come to light, in time to prevent Eleanor from becoming a bigamist. Another secret, that Sir Jesse Sullivan, Fulbert's father, has also fathered illegitimately the three Marlowes, Priscilla, Susan, and Lester, is only partially revealed.

The strongest exception to the rule that secrets are not kept is *Elders and Betters*, one of the strongest of all the novels. Anna Donne destroys her aunt Sukie's will in favour of Sukie's brother-in-law, Thomas Calderon, and his family, and preserves a later will which leaves Sukie's fortune to herself, Anna. Even worse, Anna is responsible for the death of her other aunt, Thomas's wife Jessica, having planted suspicions in Jessica's mind that her children do not love her which have led to Jessica's suicide. Neither fact is discovered; Anna emerges triumphant, both with the money and with the cousin she loves as her husband. If Anna's triumph is disturbing, it is not so much that one wants Anna punished, rather that one expects the secrets to be revealed. Yet one has a certain satisfaction at Anna's success, a feeling it may be just as well not to explore.

Magdalen Doubleday, in *Manservant and Maidservant*, wishes to marry Mortimer Lamb, the dependent cousin of Horace Lamb, the tyrant of this novel. Mortimer and Charlotte, Horace's wife, have long been in love; but when Charlotte is presumed drowned, Mortimer becomes engaged to Magdalen. Then Mortimer learns that Magdalen, in possession of a letter from Charlotte to Mortimer which reveals their love, has so arranged it that Horace will read the letter. Discovering Magdalen's scheme, Mortimer ruefully breaks off his engagement with her. There are other secrets in this novel, one the peculiar circumstance that Miss Buchanan, a village shop-keeper, cannot read. Step by step her illiteracy becomes known in the servants' hall. Though at the end Miss Buchanan's secret is known only to five people, one realizes perfectly that, in the delight of gossip and the joy of malice, it will continue to spread and spread.

In *Two Worlds and Their Ways*, the ways of the two worlds of home and school are very secretive ones. Both children of Sir Roderick and Lady Shelley, Clemence and Sefton, are discovered to have cheated at their schools, and in turn their parents' "cheating" becomes known—Maria has stolen an ear-ring, and Sir Roderick has fathered an illegitimate child, the butler Aldom. The former secret becomes known to all; the latter only limitedly public. In each novel there seem to be more and more secrets. In *Two Worlds*, Oliver Firebrace (Sir Roderick's father-in-law by his first marriage) has, like his son-in-law, fathered a son illegitimately, Oliver Spode. This fact becomes known only to Sir Roderick. That Oliver Spode has become the lover of Oliver Shelley, Sir Roderick's son by his first marriage, at the same school where Sefton met his downfall, is made more generally public. Homosexual incest is an unusual secret.

As its title indicates, *Darkness and Day* is dominated by the theme of secrets. The dark is the imagined incest between Edmund Lovat and his wife Bridget, who come to think that they are father and (illegitimate) daughter. The day is the truth: that the belief their marriage is incestuous is unfounded. Their daughter Viola's fear of the night shadows in the nursery is part of the dark-light imagery. Two other secrets that are disclosed are that Mildred Hallam is Edmund Lovat's illegitimate daughter, and that Bridget is Sir Ransom Chace's illegitimate daughter. One secret that does not generally emerge—it is known only to Mrs. Spruce, Selina Lovat's cook, and to Selina herself—is that Mrs. Spruce is Bridget's mother: so that some darkness does remain despite the general day. It is Bridget herself who remarks, what might have been said in any of the novels, "Why is it that anything against us always leaks out? I suppose when anything is in our favour, we do not wait for it to do so." Although a prodigious effort is made to keep such secrets as the suspected incest between Edmund and Bridget from leaking out, the pattern is here, as it is generally, that the secret is disclosed. So great an emphasis on secrets can make the convention seem a little creaky; for example, it is odd that all these intelligent people have not long since suspected that Sir Ransom is Bridget's father, since his special fond interest in her is so clearly paternal. Such lack of suspicion is apparent in other novels. But as an organizing theme the importance of secrets is here paramount, and its powerful interest is, here especially, very clear.

In *The Present and the Past* the tyrant Cassius Clare's tendency to deception is responsible for his death. Cassius fakes a suicide, but his infant son Toby discovers that Cassius has taken only four of the pills of which ten would have killed him. Later, Cassius dies of an actual heart attack which would not have proved mortal had he not cried wolf before; his family think that he will sleep off the present attack just as he has the earlier calculated one, and they do not call the doctor who could have saved him.

Once again in *Mother and Son* secrets are central. Here, all is revealed without exception. Hester Wolsey attempts to marry the widower Sir Julius Hume—she has acted as companion to his wife Miranda, who has now died, but it is Emma Greatheart, with whom Hester had formerly lived, that Sir Julius prefers. In a scene which seethes with her jealousy, Hester reveals that Francis, Alice, and Adrian Hume, the presumed nephews and niece of Sir Julius, are in fact his illegitimate children, and that Rosebery, the supposed son of Sir Julius who has proposed to Miss Burke (companion/housekeeper to Emma Greatheart), is in fact the illegitimate child of the dead Miranda; and had first proposed to Hester herself. As a result, no marriages take place, and the novel ends.

The tyrant in *A Father and his Fate* is Miles Mowbray. His stratagems of concealment meet with complete unsuccess. There is the usual pattern of people going away and returning. Miles and his wife Ellen go away; Ellen is presumed lost in a shipwreck; but Miles returns, and is on the verge of marrying the young and attractive Verena Gray, when Ellen also returns to England, though not to her home, not dead at all. Miles' crime is that he finds out that Ellen is alive, and even sends her money to live on, but goes ahead with his somewhat foolish plans for bigamy. Miles is the most fatuous of the tyrants, and there is a certain appealing innocence about his machinations. All of them succeed, even though all of them become public knowledge.

Simon Challoner, the hero of *A Heritage and its History*, is so intent upon inheriting his uncle Sir Edwin's estate that he seduces his uncle's wife Rhoda; the product of this union, Hamish, is taken by Sir Edwin as his heir. The truth of Hamish's parentage is disclosed when he wishes to marry Simon's daughter Naomi. Naomi is the child of Simon by his wife Fanny, who (and it seems rather needlessly complicated) is Rhoda's sister; Naomi is therefore both cousin and half-sister to Hamish. Despite his wrongdoing, despite its revelation, Simon does, in the end, come into his heritage.

The secrets in *The Mighty and Their Fall* are neatly parallel. Lavinia Middleton is so deeply attached to her father Ninian that she attempts to prevent his marriage to Teresa Chilton by concealing the letter of acceptance Teresa sends Ninian. The letter of course comes to light. Then Ninian destroys the will of his brother Ransom which would have left the latter's fortune to Lavinia instead of to himself. And once again this private act becomes public. Ninian marries Teresa, and Lavinia inherits her uncle's money.

In the last novel, *A God and his Gifts*, secrets are the core of the events. The "god" of that novel, Hereward Egerton the writer, has had a series of love affairs which are one by one, though not in chronological order, discovered: one is with Emmeline, the sister of his wife Ada, and the result of the union with Emmeline is the child Viola; another is with Hetty, the wife of his son (by Ada) Merton, and the result of this union is the child Henry; one is with Rosa Lindsay, an early mistress, a union without offspring. Hereward is also on his way to seducing Trissie, whom his son Reuben marries, but is prevented in time. Hereward's "gifts" can be seen to be more than literary. As a summary of the results of all such revelations, the following conversation between two of Hereward's sons can be recorded:

> "But he [Hereward] is to return to the heights," said Reuben. "You are to find you have never liked him so well . . ."
>
> "And it is what happens when wrong-doers are exposed," said Salomon. "I always feel I should like them less. But it seems to be unusual."

It is also Salomon who summarizes the devastation which secrets cause with the following inclusive statement, made when he learns that Viola, whom he has planned to marry, is in fact his half-sister, being the illegitimate daughter of Hereward:

> ". . . I have no wish to be revenged. You have done me no conscious wrong. But these secrets should not be. They lie beneath our life to escape and shatter it. They must be revealed and ended."

In establishing at such length the role of secrets in the novels, I have listed only those which are central to the events. But how many of minor deceptions, ruses, sly stratagems of all kinds, one could add. The war between truth and falsehood is relentless, it touches every level of conduct, it occurs every minute, whether, to use examples only from *Men and Wives*, it is Rachel Hardisty attacking the smooth self-love of Agatha Calkin or Camilla Christy remarking that Dominic Spong, whose favourite pose is that of the tragically bereft widower, has a roving eye. The following example from the same work will serve to show the persistence of minor falsehood and of the attacks on it, and the results, if they can be called that, of the attacks. Lady Haslam has suffered a mental breakdown, and Sir Godfrey, her husband, has promised that he will visit the sickroom every hour during the night to ascertain her condition. He meets his children—Matthew (who is a doctor), Jermyn, Griselda, and Gregory—at breakfast:

> "Well, does the opinion of all of you agree with mine this morning? I don't think there is much change. I can't say that I do."
>
> "The absence of mind has become almost a trance," said Matthew. "She seemed to be sleeping most of the night. I went in at three and at five. Gregory and Griselda thought she had slept. Unless she was just lying in a coma, with closed eyes. What did you think?"
>
> "Oh, well, I can hardly say. I was very exhausted," said his father, pulling back his chair with his eyes on it.
>
> "What time in the night did you first see her?" said Matthew. "I met Gregory in her room at about three. I hadn't been in until then."
>
> "Yes, yes, I think you are right. I don't think there is much difference between her state and a trance. A trance, a coma, a sort of stupor is what I should call it."
>
> "I want to know how gradually the change came on."
>
> "I can hardly say. I slept a very exhausted sleep. You think there is a definite change, then? That is what you would say?"

"Undoubtedly, by now. But I should like to tell Dufferin [Lady Haslam's doctor] when it began. What was the earliest hour you saw her?"

"When I saw her just now, I thought there was a change certainly," said Gregory.

Griselda let a sound of laughter escape.

"I wish I had the spirit to laugh," said her father, regarding her with knitted brows.

"I know how you must wish it," said Jermyn, "from being in the same situation. This is not an occasion when a night of unbroken rest makes for self-confidence in the morning."

"Oh, well, no, it is not. That is the truth about me," said Godfrey, his voice breaking out towards fullness. "I slept like a man recovering from sickness, and that in effect was what I was doing. The strain of submitting to this cannot be supported easily. Every ounce of my energy was drained out. I hadn't enough, after what I had been through, to raise my head from the pillow. It might have been me and not your mother in a trance, for all the difference there was."

And thus the battles continue, throughout all the novels. The forces are very evenly matched. Truth may triumph, and the secrets may no longer be secrets. But there will always be more secrets, human nature being what it is.

One of the psychological traits most frequently seen in action in the novels is the trait of curiosity. Its relationship to the theme of secrets is obvious and inevitable. Servants listen behind doors, and, below stairs, spend their time gossiping, not always with perfect intelligence. Governesses, tutors, companions, and others employed above stairs devote their lives to the exercise and satisfaction of their sense of inquiry; for example, we are told of Bennet, the head nurse in *The Present and the Past*, that "She took little interest in herself, and so much in other people that it tended to absorb her being." We see curiosity functioning particularly among the outsiders, those other families in the village whose life receives such interest from the secrets revealed in the life of the principal family. Curiosity is often a mark of intelligence, and it sometimes seems as if the best mental energies of the outsiders were devoted to discovering what lies hidden in the central household. Some characters, like Sarah Middleton in *A Family and a Fortune*, seem to have no other trait but curiosity; her questions, which are incessant, seem to come in spite of herself, as if her curiosity were stronger than her will; and Charity Marcon, in *Daughters and Sons*, rushes to the central household of the Ponsonby's when catastrophe is rumoured with such rapidity and is there so insistently inquiring that two or three times she is virtually evicted. Clara Bell ("Claribel") in *Elders and Betters* is a good example of the outsider who must always be "in" on things; the cousin with whom she lives, Benjamin Donne, having just learned that his sister Jessica has killed herself, says,

> "I must go to my sister's house. And my daughter and my eldest son will bear me company."
>
> He left the room with these members of his family, and Claribel strolled out after them with an expression of troubled aloofness.

Their curiosity may be vulture-like, or it may be sympathetic, but such people as Claribel refuse to be left in ignorance when aught of disaster transpires. Elizabeth Bowen has said that the characters in the novels "advance on each other's houses in groups, like bomber formations";[3] curiosity is usually what propels them.

Another related feature of the novels is the speed with which news travels. Let something occur, and the news of it passes from house to house, very often by way of the servants, with a speed considerably greater than that of sound. But just as when an accident occurs in any isolated place and dozens of spectators at once spring out of the ground, so there is a mystery to the communication of calamity. The young Mowbray cousins in *A Father and his Fate* are speaking when their aunt Eliza, who lives some distance away, appears:

> "They cannot know anything about this last—disclosure. There is no way in which they can have heard."
>
> "There is always a way," said Malcolm.
>
> Eliza's manner, when she entered, revealed that there had been a way.
>
> "My dear ones, I felt I must come to you. Why do we give our reasons? It was just that my heart went out to you, and I followed where it led."
>
> "As it was in the right direction," said Malcolm."Perhaps you can receive news from a distance like a savage."

A much more striking and prevalent convention in the novels is the presence in the dialogue of an extraordinary quantity of *sotto voce* comments. They are related to the subject under discussion in the present chapter in that they are truthful comments, often of the sharpest wit and insight, on the conduct or conversation of some other character present. They occur particularly at table, and particularly among the younger dependants of the head of a household. They are revenge, even if a powerless revenge, against his tyranny; they liberate and affirm the opposing spirit. All the distortions of motive and emphasis of which tyranny is capable meet, in these comments, with an active and intelligent antagonism.

These *sotto voce* comments are very clearly derived from the practice of the stage. In an interview between Frank Kermode and Miss Compton-Burnett which appeared in the *Partisan Review*, there is the following exchange:

> KERMODE: . . . I notice in a good many of your novels a tendency to use what in a play would be called an "aside," and not to observe the dramatic convention that the aside is never overheard; asides are always overheard in your dialogues.
>
> COMPTON-BURNETT: Yes. I think they are. I put them in to have them overheard. I don't see how you can help it if you write a book that's—in my case—something rather between a novel and a play . . . I think if you write in dialogue, things must be uttered aloud, otherwise there is no book.[4]

In actual dramatic practice asides are always heard by the audience; very rarely, they are overheard by another character on the stage; they may either be monologue (a character speaking "aside" to himself) or dialogue (two or more characters speaking "aside" among themselves). We, like the audience in a theatre, always hear the asides. But both Mr. Kermode and Miss Compton-Burnett are mistaken in thinking that the asides in her novels are always overheard by other characters. "Whispering, whispering," says Hetta Ponsonby to her nieces and nephews in *Daughters and Sons*; "always whispering." She almost never hears what they are whispering about. The term "*sotto voce* comment" is a more accurate one than "aside" because asides in drama are so often not addressed to anyone, and are merely revelatory remarks made by the speaker for his own benefit (and for the benefit of the audience); in Miss Compton-Burnett's novels the "aside" is always, without exception, addressed to another person or other persons—and, once again, may or may not be overheard. The point is worth labouring because these comments, as I have said before, are so frequent a recourse against tyranny, so psychologically apt an example of the continuous search for truth which composes the novels. The following *sotto voce* comment in *A Father and his Fate*, made by Malcolm Mowbray to his cousin Ursula, may give another reason for this pronounced feature of the dialogue:

> "Whispering!" said Miles. "Whispering and questioning! The two unforgivable things! And we seem to have nothing else."
>
> "Of course we have been whispering," said Malcolm to Ursula. "What is there about any of it fit to be uttered aloud?"

Of course to a tyrant questioning is "unforgivable," but it is sometimes the only opposition of which his victims are capable. The *sotto voce* convention occurs in all the novels, even *Dolores*; perhaps its most marked appearance is in *A House and its Head*, where it rises to a veritable babble. Not only the children of tyrants, though they are by far the most frequent, but any truth-speaking persons make use of this weapon; one thinks of that charming pair, Charity and Stephen Marcon in *Daughters and Sons*, who in the remarks they address only to each other are most energetically engaged in puncturing any pretence or hypocrisy they have observed.

The following lines from *A Heritage and its History* will show the relationship between the convention of *sotto voce* comment and another convention, that of eavesdropping:

> "You have begun to talk in low tones," said Walter, looking back. "That might be a good thing, if overhearing were not better."
>
> "The last is never wise," said Julia. "We none of us talk to people as we do behind their backs."

The custom of eavesdropping has already been mentioned in connection with the trait of curiosity. The servants of the household are given to eavesdropping not only on the family but on one another. The footman Bartle in *Darkness and Day* is not a very respectful boy; here he has been eavesdropping at the senior servants' conversation, which has taken an elevated turn:

> "I feel I have been in church," said Bartle's voice.
>
> "If you always felt that, when you had been eavesdropping, your life would have a religious bent," said Ambrose.

Another exchange between the butler and his subordinate:

> "To know all is to forgive all," said Ambrose.
>
> "Then know I have been listening at the door," said Bartle.

Some of the most brilliant effects in the novels are achieved when the two are joined, the *sotto voce* comment meeting with the eavesdropper. What was designed not to be overheard, is overheard; usually, unfortunately, by the tyrant. The first full example, too long to cite, occurs in *More Women than Men*, where, in a scene that would be marvellously effective on a stage, Josephine Napier makes an exit, and her nephew and his fiancée begin to talk about her; but she has overheard, and returns; once again makes a less-than-total exit, by which the pair she leaves are once again fooled, and she returns, to comment on what they have said to each other, and so on, till her nephew protests, "Josephine, pray come in or go out . . . We hardly understand this talking to someone neither here nor elsewhere. It is an unbearable method of communication. Do make up your mind."

As one of the girls says of her boarding school in *Two Worlds and Their Ways*, "This place is a nest of professional eavesdroppers." And of course she is overheard saying this. Sabine, the tyrant of *Daughters and Sons*, is the most unscrupulous of eavesdroppers; her daughter Hetta, a secondary tyrant, inherits the tendency. Sabine is particularly bald in gratifying her desires: she is speaking of her youngest granddaughter, Muriel:

> "She is at the age when it is usual for a child to need training," said Sabine, returning to the room with a vase of flowers, an almost recognised pretext for her appearance at any moment, versed in the conversation.

The private comment is rendered unusually perilous in *A House and its Head* by the fact that the tyrant Duncan is intermittently deaf. In the following passage he overhears a conversation concerning his overhearing propensities:

> "I can never make out whether Father's hearing is below the average or above it," said Nance.
>
> "You have made up your mind for some time," said Duncan. "It would have to be very much below, to prevent my realising it."

Thus, from the harmless amusement which the nosiness of Bartle affords to the grimness of Duncan's stern repressions, the device is everywhere. But it is more than a device. It is one of those arenas where tyranny seeks to tighten still further its heavy grasp, and where the free spirit fights back, even if its replies are unheard, with defiant wit and truth. Bergson speaks of laughter as being a corrective device for "rigidity";[5] it is the inflexibility of the tyrant by which we know him. Freud quotes Jean Paul as saying that "wit begets freedom, and freedom begets wit"; whether or not they attain a measure of freedom, it is by their wit that we know the victims of a tyrant, and his opponents.[6]

CHAPTER FOUR

PEOPLE AND POWER

"Few people can stand power."—*The Present and the Past*

I

CHARACTERIZATION. THE TYRANT

If what we most of all want from fiction is to learn about other human beings like or unlike ourselves simply because we are ourselves human beings, and if the chief standard by which we judge a novelist is his ability to create character, then the novels of Miss Compton-Burnett must rank exceptionally high. It is a bold claim, but I should say that there is no other living novelist to equal her. And what I think must finally strike us in a consideration of her characters is the differences among them, as much as their similarities.

This, in the face of the contrary view of some of her ablest critics. Pamela Hansford Johnson finds that there are "only about half a dozen people who can be remembered easily without recourse to the text or without any special searching of the memory."[1] I do not know if it is a question of fond predilection, of memory, or of some sort of subjective familiarity that I can remember at least half a dozen people from any novel that Miss Compton-Burnett has written. I hope that the present chapter, together with Chapter VI, where the novels are discussed one by one with a special emphasis on characterization, may capture some of the various rich vitality of everyone from Dominic Spong to Muriel Ponsonby, from Dulcia Bode to Emma Greatheart. But I'm not concerned especially to prove the memorability of the characters, because I don't think that such things can be proved. The novels must be read carefully, of course. And re-read.

Novel readers are often fast careless readers, quite the opposite from poetry readers; or perhaps one should say that novel-reading is apt to be much more fast and careless than poetry-reading. The cause, once again, is the abiding influence on our reading habits and expectations of the standard three-decker of a century ago. The Victorian novelist often wrote in a fast and careless manner, and he was, and is, read as he wrote. One cannot brood very productively over a page of Trollope, Thackeray is thin compared to Proust. Miss Compton-Burnett's novels demand an alert intelligence. The prevalence of the conventions which we have described, the similarities in setting and theme and wit, may mislead the rapid reader into thinking her characters are equally similar. There are indeed types of characters—the tyrant, the governess, the butler, the sophisticate, and so on: but there is a large diversity of types, and within the type no two characters are the same. One can beg the question of characterization by saying that Shakespeare returned to Falstaff, or by pointing out the repetitive types in Latin comedy, in Molière, in Corneille: and indeed in such plays characters are often so flat and familiar that they could be interchanged among the plays with no loss. But that is not the case here. Character is conceived vitally, complexly, fully. I agree with Richard Strachey who has said, "One could fill a book with commentary on the subtle differences of her characters . . ."[2] I do not agree with the reviewer of *The Mighty and Their Fall* in *The Times Literary Supplement* who wrote:

> It has been objected that Miss Compton-Burnett's novels are too much the same, in the sense that similar characters in different novels are difficult to distinguish from one another. But that she is at all concerned to create personalities in the modern manner seems unlikely. She wishes rather to reveal certain traits and impulses of human nature than to explore the idiosyncrasy of a particular person; and for this purpose the classical strictness of her conventions is ideal. The heights and depths of character are laid bare in the drawing-room; Aeschylus has been transposed into the key of Jane Austen.[3]

Interesting and ingenious though these statements are, it is my simpler opinion that the novels are full of round characters. One is tempted to list them at random (Sophia Stace, Rosebery Hume, Felix Bacon, Hetta Ponsonby, etc., etc.), not ignoring that there are similarities among them, nor forgetting that there are also numerous flat characters. I do not know of any novelist who is as thorough in the presentation of interrelationships, by which I mean each character's special attitude towards and relationship with every other character. In these novels we know who is the father's favourite child and who isn't, and why; we know every child's attitudes towards his parents, grandparents, tutor or governess or nurse; we know the wife's attitude towards her mother-in-law; we know how the members of the central family think, each in his own way, of the outsiders; and so on and on. There is an intricate network of relationships, and they of course add a lifelike depth to the characterization, as well as being of interest in themselves.

Edward Sackville-West has listed his objections to the characterization in greater detail than any other critic. Two are especially interesting:

> She cannot manage masculine men. Her males are either overtly effete (e.g. Alfred Marcon in *Daughters and Sons*), or possessed by a feline power-mania (e.g. Duncan Edgeworth in *A House and its Head*).

> Her chief characters do not develop in the course of the book, they only loom larger or dwindle, according as the author lengthens or shortens her opera-glass.[4]

First, while it is true that there are many effete men, there are many masculine men. In *Men and Wives* alone, for example, there are Matthew Haslam and Antony Dufferin; and there are men who while not markedly masculine are by no means effete: Sir Percy Hardisty and Dominic Spong. (All four of these men, incidentally, are round characters.) Second, I do not see that a power mania need be feline. There are several rigidly autocratic and sexually energetic male tyrants in the novels, and Duncan Edgeworth is one of them. Would Mr. Sackville-West call Oedipus feline? Third, as has been said before, people do not change as much in life as they do in fiction. That they do change so often in fiction, comes from the novelist's desire to impose form and meaning on the flux of experience. Moreover there is many a novel by many a writer where the chief characters do not change or develop. Two statements made by Miss Compton-Burnett in a recent interview are relevant here:

> "The action of my books, on the whole, covers a short time, so that it is hardly possible for a character to grow. It takes a long time for a human being to change."

> "I think it's very difficult to alter people, very difficult either to corrupt or improve them. The essence of people remains what it is."[5]

By their very natures the tyrants, who are the chief characters, do not change, for it is the inflexibility of their will that makes them tyrants.

The psychology of tyranny can be most closely studied in the family, and it is the family and family relations that Miss Compton-Burnett has chosen as her subject. The family allows for the great, the traditional subjects: desire for power, jealousy, war between the generations, and so on. As someone says in *A House and its Head*, "Things tend to become rooted in families." A character in *Daughters and Sons* remarks, "Life is less deep when you are not related." And it is the tutor Mr. Pettigrew in *Mother and Son* who says, "A great deal goes on beneath the surface in a family." Family life is a difficult subject for the novelist. Joyce Cary once said in an interview:

> "Family life, no. Family life just goes on. Toughest thing in the world. But of course it is also the microcosm of a world. You get everything there—birth, life, death, love and jealousy, conflict of wills, of authority and freedom, the new and the old."[6]

The novels depict all the close family relationships, and sometimes the relationships become too close. There is the tie between mother and son, which ends in disaster in *Men and Wives*, where Harriet Haslam is killed by her son Matthew. There is the bond between two brothers, which is studied in the figures of Edgar and Dudley Gaveston in *A Family and a Fortune*, and most of all in *A Heritage and its History*, where we are told of Hamish Challoner that "His brother [Sir Edwin] had always been the centre of his life" and where Hamish's sons, Simon and Walter, also have a very close accord. The closeness of father and daughter is often apparent, and is quite important in *The Mighty and Their Fall*, where Lavinia tries to prevent her father's remarriage. In the last novel, *A God and his Gifts*, the hero Hereward, who is well on his way towards the seduction of his prospective daughter-in-law Hetty, says to her:

> "Ah, I should have had a daughter. I have always known it."
>
> "You will have one now. And you will have others through your other sons."
>
> "I only want one. It is what I need. It is the classic relation, rooted in the past. My wife has done much for me. But now [she has done] all she can do. And my sons go their distance, and can go no further."

Mother and daughter are best seen in *Daughters and Sons*, where the pretended suicide of Hetta Ponsonby causes the decline and death of her aged parent, Sabine Ponsonby. But the relationship the most frequently and closely analysed is that of brother and sister. There are Stephen and Charity Marcon in *Daughters and Sons*, John and Hetta Ponsonby in the same novel, and many more; most of all in the early novel *Brothers and Sisters*. It is again in the last novel, *A God and his Gifts*, however, that the most inclusive statement is made:

> "Zillah, we are brother and sister. If we were not, what could we be?"
> "Nothing that was nearer. It stands first among the relations. There is nothing before it, nothing to follow it. It reaches from the beginning to the end."

Hereward, as something in the tone of his voice will indicate, looms large as a person. One of the most scrupulously employed among Miss Compton-Burnett's powers of characterization is her ability to make us feel the relative weight of such people as Hereward. What quality is it that gives a man or women this special dominance, forcefulness, size as a personality? Is it his intelligence, his single-mindedness, his being more what he is than other people are what they are—that is, his *quidditas*, or *whatness*? It may be any or all of these, or any number of other traits; but surely one of our best-employed instincts in life is the ability to recognize the person on a large scale, and I think that we feel the absence of this discrimination in a novel where the characters have the same tone or intensity or dimensions. Ibsen had to an extraordinary degree the ability to make us feel the relative weight of his characters. Jane Austen had it also. One of the disappointing things about James Baldwin's novel *Another Country* is that all his people are of the same density. In life people are so often major or minor. In a novel like *Elders and Betters*, Anna is major and Claribel is minor. In *The Mighty and Their Fall*, Selina Middleton has tried to prevent the marriage of her adopted son Hugo to her granddaughter Lavinia:

> "I wanted to save you," said Selina, in a deeper tone, leaning forward and looking into her face. "Hugo does not care for you enough. You are a person who inspires deep feeling. That is a thing we don't explain. He has not the depth in him that you have."

"That is a thing we don't explain": whatever the quality that causes the depth that Selina speaks of, it is the principal trait of the principal characters of these novels.

Although we have said that no two characters are the same, it is convenient to consider them by groups or types. One can do this with any author without denying the final individuality of his creations. Because of the numerous conventions employed in these novels, with the milieu usually limited to a house or two, and with the main household being of a certain class, there are bound to be repetitive occupations—tutors and butlers, companions and cooks. And I think it is well to point out, what sometimes is forgotten, that there is a family resemblance among any novelist's characters; that is, all Dostoevsky's characters are recognizably Dostoevskyan, all Dickens' characters are recognizably Dickensian, and so forth. To prove the point one need only to try to imagine a character of Hemingway's in a novel by Kafka. Miss Compton-Burnett's characters are her own characters and not any one else's.

The central figures in Miss Compton-Burnett's novels are the power figures, or tyrants, and some of their traits have already been mentioned. For one thing, it is the tyrants who have the secrets and who attempt to suppress the truth; for another, they are people who "loom large." They are the people with "a strong grip on life"; they are the people with power.

Power is a keyword to the novels. The implications of power are considered from innumerable standpoints. It is made the essential distinction between people in the following conversation of two candid wise children in *The Mighty and Their Fall*:

> "She [their governess] means our level is low," said Leah.
> "Well, so is everyone's. Only some people have more power. People are really the same."

Of the desire for power, Ursula Scrope, in *The Present and the Past*, says:

> "People think it natural to want power, and wrong to exercise it."

Another epigram, spoken by Griselda Haslam about her tyrannical mother in *Men and Wives*:

> ". . . We tremble before signs that she is tempted to use her power. People can't have so much without its occurring to them to use it."

And another, spoken by Mortimer Lamb to his cousin Horace Lamb, the tyrant of *Manservant and Maidservant*:

> "You are in a beautiful place. I do not wonder you talk about it. It must

> be wonderful to have power, and use it with moderation and cruelty. We can so seldom be admired and self-indulgent at the same time."

Over and over the bad effects of power are stated and shown. Sophia Stace, in *Brothers and Sisters*, before her father has died and she has assumed his place as family tyrant, says, with what turns out to be premonitory irony:

> "I would not stoop to use absolute power like that. It shows how degrading absolute power can be."

Power is respected, as the Reverend Dr. Chaucer learns in a conversation with two of the Ponsonby children in *Daughters and Sons*:

> "Victor," said Chaucer with a hesitant air, "you will allow me my word? You will remember your grandmother is a very old lady, and, as such, as entitled to your chivalry as she is dependent upon it. We show honour to the weaker vessel."
>
> "We do not show honour to Grandma in that character," said Clare. "Hers is the honour paid to power. And it is a better kind of honour."

And power is always active, not passive. Gabriel Swift says to his aunt Josephine Napier, the tyrant in *More Women than Men*:

> "You are such a powerful person, that it seems to be right that you should use your power. . . ."

Omnipotence is an attribute of God, and the power figure is apotheosized as God in the last two novels, *The Mighty and Their Fall* and *A God and his Gifts*. In the former book Hugo Middleton is speaking to his adoptive brother, the tyrant Ninian:

> "I have never believed in God. I believe in him now. We have known he is a father. And I see that he is yours. There are the anger, jealousy, vaingloriousness, vengefulness, love, compassion, infinite power. The matter is in no doubt."

In these novels there is almost never a case of power being used for the good of others. Its fatal selfishness is recognized by the Ponsonby children in *Daughters and Sons*:

> "Grandma is the only one of us in a strong position," said Chilton. "She cannot be sent into her grave out of due time."
>
> "It would be good to have power," said his brother.
>
> "No, we should use it," said France. "No one can stand it. None of us could: think of the stock we come of."

That power corrupts is a familiar idea. A less familiar insight, of bold and profound interest, is that power attracts. It is a case of "unto every one that hath shall be given, and he shall have abundance." Even though a tyrant's dependants recognize the attraction his power exercises, they are nonetheless susceptible to it. The Spanish poet Lorca recognizes this in the formidable appeal of Bernarda Alba. As in Lorca's play, in Miss Compton-Burnett's novels the defences of a tyrant's victims are weakened by the fascination he arouses. Camilla Christy says about Harriet Haslam in *Men and Wives*, "She is a high-minded old tyrant. I quite adore her." It is the superb Bullivant, the butler in *Manservant and Maidservant*, who has the final word on the subject in a conversation with Mortimer Lamb, who says to Bullivant:

> "My life is settled for me, and I have accepted it. Do you think we have acquired a taste for despotic dealing?"
>
> "Well, it has comprised our experience, sir; we might as well say we had acquired a taste for life itself."

To generalize about the traits of a tyrant, those features of personality by which we know him, one notices at the outset that, in contrast to such likeable persons as Mortimer Lamb, the power figure is without charm. Only Hereward Egerton in *A God and his Gifts*, among all the tyrants, has that unique and immediate appeal, although charm is a quality much prized and practised in the novels. Of the tyrant Hetta Ponsonby in *Daughters and Sons*, we are told:

> Hetta made an effort to retrieve her position, and talked with the conscious fluency and liveliness which she felt to be charm . . .

But Hetta is unsuccessful in her attempt, because there is that darker and harsher side of her nature which cannot be repressed. Another trait, which in itself precludes the possibility of charm, and one that is pronounced in Hetta, is that the tyrant always attacks. Here is the beginning of *Daughters and Sons*; the tyrant is Hetta's mother Sabine, from whom Hetta has inherited her drive to dominate:

> "Well, gapy-face," said Mrs. Ponsonby.
>
> A girl of eleven responded to this morning greeting.
>
> "I wasn't yawning, Grandma."
>
> "Do not lie to me, child; do not lie; do not begin the day by lying," said Sabine Ponsonby, entering her dining-room and glancing rapidly round it. "And it would be better to shut your mouth and open your eyes. You will have us confusing one part of your face with the other."

These dominant people are dominated by their own idea of themselves, a sense of their own importance which, among their most aggressive members, is vividly and boldly stated. Here is Sophia Stace, in *Brothers and Sisters*, whose husband has just paid her a compliment:

> "Ah, you will never get to the end of finding what I can do," said Sophia with a flash of her eyes. "You will always go on discovering that. I sometimes find myself marvelling at the gulf between the average person and myself."

After the death of her husband, Sophia addresses their children:

> "We will go apart, and try to meet together our great, great sorrow. Great for you all, but infinitely greater for me. You will have to remember that, in all your future dealings with me."

Even more succinct is Matty Seaton in *A Family and a Fortune*, speaking to her companion Miss Griffin:

> "I am a very exceptional person and in a tragic position, and you will have to grasp it, or you are no good to me."

And Hereward Egerton in *A God and his Gifts* says simply, "I know I am built on a large scale." The self-esteem of the tyrants recalls that of Theobald Pontifex in Butler's *The Way of All Flesh*, a novel which has other resemblances to the present works. This egocentricity is related to the characteristic of a certain simplicity or single-mindedness, which all the tyrants without exception have. The protagonists in Greek tragedies have this quality to excess—Oedipus and Antigone and Medea, for example. As Ransom Middleton says of his brother Ninian, the tyrant of *The Mighty and Their Fall*, when he sees Ninian succumbing without hesitation to temptation:

> "Too simple . . . Too simple to hold any reason. But people who have power respond simply. They have no minds but their own."

Some of the central figures are physically afflicted, but there is no suggestion made that their tyranny serves as a psychological compensation for the affliction. Two of them are lame, one is somewhat deaf, one has a weak heart, several are in extreme old age; but the vigour of their conduct makes us think of them as physically vigorous.

Whatever else they have, they have a big capacity for love. It may not be directed towards their spouses; although Sophia Stace in *Brothers and Sisters* loves her husband—who is also her half-brother—deeply, the tyrant in another early novel, Josephine Napier in *More Women than Men*, has long since lost her love and even interest in her husband Simon, and we hear of his "resigned, but settled hopelessness." Of Sabine Ponsonby's marriage in *Daughters and Sons* we are told:

> Sabine always dressed as a widow in tribute to her husband, who was entitled to this amount of recognition, as he had been an excellent man, and was accorded no other. Sabine had regarded him first as her husband, then as her subject, and since his death as a conventional character, unrelated to the truth.

But typically these large-scale people have large-scale loves, particularly the love of their children. The first example that comes to mind is Harriet Haslam in *Men and Wives*, whose love for her children is accompanied, as in life it often is, by proportionately high demands on them. The relation between love and power is shown in the following dialogue between the child Venice Sullivan and her governess Miss Mitford in *Parents and Children*:

> "You are as afraid of Mother as we are, Mitta," said Venice.
>
> "Not quite. She has no affection for me, and that puts me outside her power."

Tyranny can descend from generation to generation (from Sabine Ponsonby to her daughter Hetta in *Daughters and Sons*, for example; Hetta's voice sometimes takes on the "piercing note" of Sabine's), can persist after death (Sabine; or Harriet Haslam in *Men and Wives*; or Miranda Hume in *Mother and Son*), can even be found in children (Nevill Sullivan in *Parents and Children*—he is only three!—is the first of the child tyrants). There are studies of incipient tyrants (Verena Gray in *A Father and his Fate*). But those adults who are established maintain their position ruthlessly; the hungry generations try to tread them down, but they do not succeed.

With each succeeding novel money becomes more closely identified with power. Money is short in the central household, and its master has the habit of pointing out the expense of his dependants' upkeep, which both incites and makes shameful their rebellion against him. As the title indicates, money is paramount in *A Family and a Fortune*; equally important in *The Mighty and Their Fall*, where Selina Middleton bequeaths money to her adopted son Hugo so that he will not marry her granddaughter Lavinia, who has in turn been left money by her uncle Ransom; and he does not. Anna Donne, in *Elders and Betters*, says:

> "I begin to think that anything to do with money, be it wills or anything else, is so considered and dwelt upon and turned this way and that in people's thoughts, that no word like rashness or impulse is ever in place."

The tyrant and indeed almost everyone else hang on to money grimly. No one gives it away, except the kindly Dudley, in *A Family and a Fortune*, and he learns to his double cost the effect of such gifts.

In fact the notion of self-sacrifice of any kind is everywhere ridiculed. It is the opposite of the power mania of the tyrant. The following exchange is between the two old friends Gaunt Lovat and Sir Ransom Chace in *Darkness and Day*:

> "I don't feel my life has been wasted."
>
> "If you have lived for others, it has. People do not want other people's lives. They think too little of them in comparison with their own."

Edith Hallam, in *Daughters and Sons*, says that "Sacrifice does recoil on people." Three wise spinsters in *Mother and Son* discuss the subject:

> "I never know why self-sacrifice is noble," said Miss Burke. "Why is it better to sacrifice oneself than someone else?"
>
> "It is no better," said Hester, "and it is not really held to be."
>
> "It does not seem we ought to matter ourselves as much as other people," said Emma. "But I have never met a case of self-sacrifice."

The French critic Raymond Las Vergnas has seen the question of self-sacrifice in these novels in the largest terms:

> Le héros est celui qui, épicuriennement accordé à l'essentiel de ses penchants, suit paisiblement le cours de sa destinée. Celui, au contraire, qui delibérément se sacrifie aux autres ne doit s'attendre à aucune récompense. Sa deception serait d'ailleurs meritée. La mutilation qu'il s'impose est absurde. Le crime fondamental est le péché contre l'esprit: la stupidité. Le reste n'est que convulsion passagère qui s'inscrit dans le fil des jours sans en altérer le tissu.[7]

One hopes that in this discussion of the traits common to tyranny we have not lost sight of the fact that no two of the tyrants are the same. From the sincerity and love of Harriet Haslam to the ruthless lies and self-adulation of Josephine Napier, from the tired old virulence of Sabine Ponsonby to the bland egotism of Hereward Egerton, the dominant people are individuals, alike in the way that certain types of people can be alike, but no more alike than that. Each has his lively diversity, and each has his diverse effect upon us.

II

CHILDREN

The chief victims of the tyrant are his children. The children in Miss Compton-Burnett's works have been a favourite subject for her critics, who have found them "frightening" and "fascinating" and "astonishingly adult." It is true that they are precocious. The two most precocious are Rose Lovat, who is ten, in *Darkness and Day*, and Megan Clare, who is seven, in *The Present and the Past*. Megan is preposterous.

But all the children are children. Though they are often faultlessly articulate, their candour and directness and intelligence allow them to be, just as they do, if rarely, in real life. There is as much variety among them as there is among the adults; they are miniature tyrants like Nevill Sullivan in *Parents and Children*, or they are odd perplexed small creatures like Henry Clare in *The Present and the Past*. How pathetic they can be, like Aubrey Gaveston in *A Family and a Fortune*, who is a boy of fifteen, small for his age; sensitive and shy, yet wry and witty and intelligent; victimized by a cruel older brother, Clement. Aubrey somewhat resembles the appealing boy Reuben Donne in *Elders and Betters*. In Reuben's cousins Julius and Dora Calderon, eleven and ten respectively, who worship their strange god Chung and his son Sung-Li, all the fantasy of childhood is seen. What all the children have in common, except the very young, is what psychologists call a sense of insecurity. In the following conversation from *Parents and Children*, the speakers are Gavin, who is nine, Isabel, who is fifteen, their adult brother Graham and their grandmother Regan. Gavin makes his remark quite suddenly:

> "I should like to die," said Gavin, looking round the table.
>
> "Why would you?" said Regan and Graham at once.
>
> "Because as long as you are alive, things can happen that you don't like. Even if you couldn't bear them, they would happen."
>
> "A good description of life," said Isabel.

Even more precocious are the victim-children of Horace Lamb in *Manservant and Maidservant*, whose favourite reading is the Book of Job. At one point Marcus, who is only eleven, says: "I have thought it might be best to die . . . and now I know it would." In *The Present and the Past*, Cassius Clare says of his children, "The age of innocence! . . . It ought to be called something else." But their lack of innocence does not make them less to be pitied. One of the students at the girls' school in *Two Worlds and Their Ways* makes a request of the school matron:

> "I wish you would . . . sit with us until we are asleep," said Gwendolen. "This harsh bringing-up will make hard women of us. We shall want other people to suffer as we have."

It is a succinct statement of how and why the victims may become tyrants in their turn.

But most of the time it is the older children who bear the brunt of the tyrants' attacks. The younger children are to a degree indulged, as younger children are; but those who have reached young adulthood are spared nothing. There is often an elder daughter, like Nance Edgeworth in *A House and its Head* or Clare Ponsonby in *Daughters and Sons*, who is made a main target, whose aggressive efforts to protect her younger sisters and brothers are pathetic, whom one can see as a tall pale girl with a strained countenance and tight lips, austere of mien and shabby of garment. Another type of the elder daughter, found in the middle novels, is a bossy and energetic young woman who tries to dominate the household; there are Justine Gaveston in *A Family and a Fortune*, Luce Sullivan in *Parents and Children*, Anna Donne in *Elders and Betters*. There are several cases of a younger daughter depicted as an insincere, pretty girl, self-conscious, vain, and shallow—Sibyl Edgeworth in *A House and its Head*, Venice Sullivan in *Parents and Children*, Tullia Calderon in *Elders and Betters*.

The children tend to stick closely together, forming little phalanxes according to their age groups. The sisters are more friendly with one another than the brothers are; there are instances of rivalry among the boys, of patronizing and bullying. Both Victor Ponsonby in *Daughters and Sons* and Daniel Sullivan in *Parents and Children* mock and deride their younger brothers, Chilton and Graham respectively, though not without affection in either case. The defences of all the children against their tyrant elders have been described earlier, in

Chapter III: their constant *sotto voce* comments, their brave wit and mockery.

III

SOPHISTICATES

Neither power figures nor their victims, often cast as outsiders to the central family and acting as a chorus of comment upon it, are those characters whom, for want of a better name, we can call the sophisticates. We could also call them cynics, or anti-tyrants, if the "anti" is taken more in its sense of "opposite to" than in its sense of "one who opposes." The opposition is more intellectual than personal. At the end of Chapter II, in connection with the discussion of the role of secrets in the novels, these characters were described as truth-seekers and truth-speakers. Trissie, in *A God and his Gifts*, when asked if she always speaks the truth, replies, "If I can. Then there is nothing to remember. And words mean something."

Words mean a great deal to the sophisticates. They sometimes appear conscious of their wit to the point of intoxication, reeling off their paradoxes with an energy comic in itself. They have their humorous obsessions, like Juliet Cassidy's, in *Two Worlds and Their Ways*, about the extreme taciturnity of her husband Lucius. They are their own best audience.

This type of character never seems as fully flesh and blood as the tyrant does: not that his portrait lacks depth, but that he lacks that "relative weight of personality" which we have spoken of as a leading trait of the tyrant. The sophisticates are often effete, if they are men; spinsterish, if they are women. Their wit is opposite to the tyrant's grimness, their lightness opposite to his heaviness.

They are also opposite to him in that he acts, while they observe. They may be more intelligent than he is, but the very quickness of their minds serves to preclude action; not for them the big deed and conspicuous conduct. They have no power, but they have charm; the tyrant is the exact antithesis. The attraction they exercise is one of amusement, not of awe.

But one takes them seriously, even if they are never solemn. Their facetiousness is only the vehicle of the truths they speak, not in itself the end: they work in paradoxes. Though they do not dictate the course of events, they comprehend them better than those that do.

They appear in every novel, and one cannot imagine the novels without them, for their brilliance lights the whole.

IV

FOOLS AND FAKES

Particularly in the early novels there is a type of minor character who, unless the damage he does to the truth can be held against him, is generally harmless; who, through what is finally a lack of intelligence, adopts one pose or another; who, in his lack of resilience and imagination, is a fool. Sir Godfrey Haslam in *Men and Wives* is something of a fool, as almost any speech of his will show, but the two best examples are Peter Bateman in *Brothers and Sisters* and Clara Bell ("Claribel") in *Elders and Betters.* Peter is a remarkable creation; he is garrulous, silly, ineffectual, prying, self-deluding, insensitive, obtrusive, tactless:

> "What? What is that?" said Peter. "Monopolising the talk! Oh, have I? Tilly, why didn't you tell me? Ha, ha! Why, I don't think I have been chattering so much. You are not used to hearing me; that is it. I am one for the enjoyment of other people's conversation."

Claribel, with her lively curiosity, her vanity, her unimportance, and her mouth opened as if about to scream, is equally funny:

> "We are all about the same height," went on Claribel, "Jessica and Sukey and me. I know I ought to say 'I,' but somehow my lips do not take to that little word. I am at one with Cleopatra there. I often discover in myself an affinity with the characters that we know as friends. I wonder if she was as high as we are. We shall make quite an imposing group, if we are seen about together."

The fake is not quite so harmless. He is a more frequent type. There are several clergymen, pious frauds and hypocrites that they are, who belong in this category. There are a couple of what could be called literary fakes, Mrs. Christy in *Men and Wives*, and that fine old figure who fancies a resemblance between herself and George Eliot, Gertrude Doubleday in *Manservant and Maidservant.* Agatha Calkin in *Men and Wives*, with her constant claims to a profound knowledge of life, is especially invidious. That bouncing lass Dulcia Bode in *A House and its Head* is the supreme example of the type. All the aforementioned make use of an open air and a manner of frank and reasonable avowal, especially when they are lying. Later examples are less humorous; in *Parents and Children* we know of Ridley Cranmer's essential cheapness by his incessant use of high-sounding clichés; in *Mother and Son*, Rosebery Hume is equally incapable of sincere statement, but he is more likeable than any of his predecessors. In the late novels the type disappears or is merged with other types.

I think the fakes are more than Dickensian inheritance, more than the product of the liveliest sense of comedy. Less than honest, less than sincere, and less than highly intelligent, they are, in their different way from that of the tyrants, concealers of the truth. Lack of integrity prevails on all levels, from the highest down, as the existence of the Gertrude Doubledays and the Ridley Cranmers shows.

V

AND OTHERS

The tyrant victimizes whomever he can, and the companion, a frequent character in the novels, often serves when family fails as substitute outlet for the tyrant's wrath. Characters like Miss Patmore in *Brothers and Sisters*, Miss Griffin in *A Family and a Fortune*, Miss Jennings in *Elders and Betters*, though quite different women, are similar in their long-suffering patience and humility, their goodness and their self-effacement. What compensates for their proximity to the tyrant's bad temper is their proximity to the most intimate family affairs; curiosity is a trait in all of them. We are told of Miss Jennings that her curiosity "did not fail in any human matter."

Another and more common dependent member of the household is the governess. "Why do we feel that governesses are not like other people?" asks Ursula Scrope in *The Present and the Past.* The governesses themselves are made to feel that they are not. Underpaid and underfed by their employers, they are also the victims of the children they teach. The longest-suffering of the whole tribe is Miss Starkie, slave to the children Hengist and Leah in *The Mighty and Their Fall.* The following is typical of Hengist's and Leah's frontal assaults:

> "You haven't even any parents."
> "Well, they did not live to be old."
> "Did your being a governess break their hearts?"

> "And bring their grey hairs with sorrow to the grave?" said Leah. "That would have been a pity, if they weren't even grey."

There are some governesses in the novels, however, who are a match for their infernal charges, and there are two attributes which make them so: intelligence and a private income.

Other traits that other characters, when grouped by occupation, share in common, could be mentioned; the dignity and rhetoric of butlers and the nosiness of tutors, the aplomb of cooks and the aspirations of footmen could be described. But these are less common characters and less true to type. And what should be emphasized once again is that despite the frequency of types, no two tyrants or victims, governesses or butlers, are the same. Moreover the novels are full of fine unique studies, many of which are described in the discussions of the novels in Chapter VI. My own favourite among the minor people is the peerless Bertha Mullet, nursemaid to the youngest among the nine Sullivan children in *Parents and Children*. There is no one like her in the other novels or anywhere else. Bertha, who is described as "a freckled, healthy-looking girl of twenty-two, with eyes and hair and brows of the same fox-red colour, and something foxlike in the moulding of her face," has delusions of grandeur. I quote her at length, not only for the interest of it, but as final testimony to the wonderfully rich creation of character throughout all eighteen novels:

> "Yes, I will give you the last chapter of my childhood," said Mullet, entering on an evidently accustomed and congenial task, with her eyes and hands on Honor's head. "For I don't think I was ever a real child after that. You know we lived in a house something like this; a little smaller and more compact, perhaps, but much on the same line. And I was once left behind with the servants when my father was abroad. Not with a grandpa and a grandma and a mother; just with servants, just with the household staff. And I found myself alone in the schoolroom, with all the servants downstairs. I was often by myself for hours, as I had no equal in the house, and I preferred my own company to that of inferiors. Well, there I was sitting, in my shabby, velvet dress, swinging my feet in their shabby, velvet shoes; my things were good when they came, but I was really rather neglected; and there came a ring at the bell, and my father was in the house. 'And what is this?' he said, when he had hastened to my place of refuge. 'How comes it that I find my daughter alone and unattended?' The servants had come running up when they heard his ring, when his peremptory ring echoed through the house. 'Here is my daughter,

my heiress, left to languish in solitude! In quarters more befitting a dog,' he went on, looking round the rather battered schoolroom, and saying almost more than he meant in the strength of his feelings. 'Cast aside like a piece of flotsam and jetsam,' he continued, clenching his teeth and his hands in a way he had. 'When I left her, as I thought, to retainers faithful to the charge of my motherless child. Enough,' he said. 'No longer will I depend on those whose hearts do not beat with the spirit of trusty service. People with the souls of menials,' he went on, lifting his arm with one of his rare gestures, 'away from the walls which will shelter my child while there is breath within me.' And there he stood with bent head, waiting for the servants to pass, almost bowing to them in the way a gentleman would, feeling the wrench of parting with people who had served him all his life." Mullet's voice changed and became open and matter-of-fact. "And there we both were, left alone in that great house, with no one to look after us, and very little idea of looking after ourselves. It was a good thing in a way, as the crash had to come, and I think Father felt it less than he would have in cold blood. He was a man whose hot blood was often a help to him." Mullet gave a sigh and moved her brows. "But I think his death was really caused by our fall from our rightful place."

CHAPTER FIVE

ETHOS

"I am appalled by the threat and danger of life."
—*A Family and a Fortune*

I

THE TRAGIC

What is basic to all conceptions of tragedy is the opposition of an individual human being to some huge undefeatable force. The force is usually external; it may be Job's Jehovah, who has clothed the neck of the horse with thunder, or Atropos, who slits the thin-spun life, or Society itself, the vast mechanical monster who kills the solitary ordinary human hero of our times like Willy Loman. Sophocles, the quintessential Greek, assumed the dignity of man, the possible heroism of achievement and suffering—the one not to be separated from the other; most modern tragedians still assume, if not dignity and stature and the elevated mode, some essential fine spirit in man which confronts a social or religious circumstance; and in this confrontation there is expressed some human hope. Tragedy is always optimistic, in that human beings are seen as capable; as most interesting in their despair; as talented in their meeting it. As if the human were not enough there must be something for the human to pit itself against and prove itself more human.

Euripides is the most modern of the Greeks, and more modern than many of the moderns, in that he sees the force against which human nature struggles as internal rather than external, and the divided nature of man, who is not always pictured as noble or dignified, as the battleground. In the *Hippolytus* it is the mighty opposites of lust and chastity which occasion the misfortune and its meaning. The force is not some god, unless in the sense of Phaedra's nurse: "Aphrodite is no goddess! No! . . . —She is something more than a goddess—something greater!"[1]

The conception of tragedy which conceives of no external force, instead discerning that in our own mixed nature the elements tragically war, is the most useful means of defining the tragic content of the novels of Miss Compton-Burnett. The only point I should like to try to make about the novels as tragedies is that they are Euripidean, not Sophoclean; that they do not emphasize dignity or nobility, heroism or suffering, God or Fate; that the psychological essence of man is in itself the tragedy. This may be to leave tragedy, as it is usually thought of, behind altogether, and I do not know but what it is stretching the usual definitions of tragedy beyond useful bounds to call any of Euripides' plays tragedies. I would call them human dramas, and I would call Miss Compton-Burnett's books the same. But she is not altogether the same as Euripides; she is less sympathetic, she lacks his "warm human tears," she is more objective and detached, unambiguous and final, than he.

Her novels have been much talked of in terms of tragedy, and they themselves talk of it so much that the tendency among critics has been to assume they are attempts to write tragedy in Edwardian dress. A refinement of error, in my opinion, is to think of them as Sophoclean rather than as Euripidean. It has been fashionable to discuss them in terms of "evil," that still fashionable word; one reviewer found the last novel, *A God and his Gifts*, weak because the sense of evil was lacking. These novels are not by Dostoevsky; there is no intense Christian allegory of the satanic and the divine. There is instead the profoundly rational observation that human nature is capable of both good and bad. "Evil," as the word is literarily used, is irrational.

It is only in the Euripidean sense of tragedy, a sense so limited that, as we have said, it may be useless, that "tragedy" is a keyword to the novels. The word itself appears over and over. But its frequency varies from novel to novel; I do not believe it is mentioned in *Two Worlds and Their Ways*, while in the following novel, *Darkness and Day*, it appears at least a dozen times. The former is a lighter and shallower work, the latter grips us. I should add at once that most readers would prefer *Two Worlds* to *Darkness and Day*, because it is so much funnier. However, the point here is that one notices that certain of the novels have a deeper effect: and the question is, can one gauge the effect by the number of times "tragedy" or "tragic" is mentioned? *Pastors and Masters* is no more than a charming first book; its successor *Brothers and Sisters* is a powerful one. There is one mention of tragedy in *Pastors and Masters*; there are at least a dozen mentions in *Brothers and Sisters*. I do not find the word at all in the last novel, *A God and his Gifts*; it is the mildest of all the mature novels. What causes the variation? Is it that in some books the author's sense of tragedy as we have defined it, the recognition of the opposed elements in human nature, is more operative? But why should it be? We cannot know, but any attempt at an answer would have to take into account the author's biographical and emotional history, and also the rhythmic action and reaction which are characteristic of any artist's creativity—such as, for example, the way Beethoven's symphonies alternate between the traditional and the more boldly exploratory. In the case of the present novels all one can say is that the frequency of the word "tragedy" is a guide to the depth and intensity of the psychology.

"Comedy has tragedy behind it," says Rachel Hardisty in *Men and Wives*. The remark can tempt us to another formula: to equate wit and catastrophe, and to say that the starker the events the more glittering the play of paradox. But the truth is that the proportions of comedy and (Euripidean) tragedy are more arbitrary, and one must again take refuge behind the barricades of biography—some of the novels are more comic than others because the author's life lent itself during their composition to a happier creativity.

The traditional tragic paraphernalia are in these novels extrinsic rather than intrinsic. If they are not of the essence, of what use are they? The sophisticate Julian Wake in *Brothers and Sisters* says that "Tragedy is by far the best background, and every one behaves well in it; it is so worth while." Julian's point is that everyone does not behave well. Tragic circumstances are provided in which the participants do not behave tragically. Everywhere the traditional heavy implications of the word "tragedy" and its associated vocabulary are inverted for purposes of ironic comedy. In one sense the novels are an attack on those ideas of human nature which have made tragedy possible; they establish the tragic situation in order to demonstrate how little capable of dignity or heroism or spiritual glory people really are. Here is a brilliant couple, Helen and Felix Bacon, in *More Women than Men*:

> "Neighbours don't seem to hold the Greek view of the nobility of suffering."
>
> "Neighbours are English," said Felix.
>
> "There is no disgrace in honest poverty."

"You can't really think that. There is no point in being too Greek."

Or, in *Darkness and Day*, Gaunt Lovat, speaking of his sister-in-law Bridget to his mother Selina, says:

> "Bridget has done and suffered the traditional tragic things. As nearly the same as Oedipus, as a woman could. He killed his father and married his mother. And she caused her mother's death when she was born, and married her father. The difference is, as she said herself, that she has not put out her eyes."
>
> "Perhaps we are fortunate," said Selina drily. "Or perhaps fashions have changed."

A Heritage and its History is very rich in dramatic irony, and in references to it, but once again the characteristic tone is detached and conscious and different from the Greeks. Walter Challoner says at one point of family events:

> "It was like a Greek tragedy. . . . With people saying things with a meaning they did not know, or with more meaning than they knew."

No matter how deliberate the parallels to familiar Greek situations, as in *Darkness and Day*, the net effect is never that of Sophoclean or Shakespearean tragedy. The heroism and glory are altogether lacking. The references to tragedy often seem consciously literary. Too rational for glory, too shrewd for heroism, the novels employ the Greek paraphernalia just as they employ any other convention, as a vehicle not as an end. The novels are not tragedies in the Aristotelian definition any more than Euripides' plays are. The view of human nature is too close and too complex. In these novels, as in Greek tragedies, and as in life, some people are better or worse than others, but the author's grasp of human nature is too daily and alert to admit of a grand and elevated stylization of vices and virtues. There is too much common sense for tragedy, too pessimistic or too detailed an idea of personality. So much less even than in Euripides are the possibilities of right action emphasized. Most of all, the events are not seen in any external framework, divine or other. Some readers may find the outlook limited or harsh, and it might be this, were it not for the conclusive intelligence that so obviously is everywhere operating. Even when we are aware of deliberate Greek echoes, as we are in the chorus of schoolmistresses (Luke, Rosetti, Munday, and Chattaway) in *More Women than Men*, there is always a difference:

"It had not struck me," said Miss Luke; "had it struck any of you—that Mrs. Napier is a tragic figure?"

"Yes, it had struck me," said Miss Rosetti, idly.

A Greek chorus on occasion may become lyric, profound, etc., but it never makes any comment idly.

Hamlet says,

> But I have that within which passeth show,
> These but the trappings and the suits of woe.

The trappings of these novels, the innumerable references to "tragedy" and the obvious parallels to the familiar Greek concern with incest and pride and power might at first persuade us that they are an attempt—in the peculiar form of a dialogue novel set in an English country house of the 1890's—to re-create Greek tragedy. How banal most modern "Greek tragedies" are. The present novels are the opposite of banal, and they are not heroic, and they have another kind of power, the power of their form and wit and knowledge of human nature. It may sound unflattering to say that if the author were concerned to write Greek tragedies she would know more about them. All the references to Greek tragedy presume no more knowledge of it on our part or the author's than any sixth-former would have. We are spared the obscurities of *The Family Reunion* (that beautiful play). "There is no point in being too Greek." We are given instead a view of life which V. S. Pritchett has called, in a fine phrase, "the grave misanthropy and humility of the rationalist."[2]

II

THE RELIGIOUS

Attacks on the idea of self-sacrifice are frequent in the novels, as we have said at some length in Chapter IV. The idea of self-sacrifice is a Christian concept, one so important that Matthew Arnold in *Hebraism and Hellenism* found it the doctrine which replaced for all Christianity the Law of the Hebrews as the essential guide to conduct.

Self-sacrifice is only one aspect of the official religious belief of our culture which is assaulted in the novels of Miss Compton-Burnett.

The tone when religion is mentioned verges on strident mockery. Earlier we have given examples of the clergymen among the novels, and seen how they are variously fools or hypocrites or plain atheists. Just as Ernest Pontifex rebels against his family's beliefs and mores in *The Way of All Flesh*, the younger or shrewder members of these late-Victorian and Edwardian families make the lingering vestiges of the old attitudes the subject for irreverent wit. Some of the tyrant figures, especially in the early novels, are religious; Harriet Haslam in *Men and Wives*, for example. She has some sort of fundamentalist belief, though the usual range of religious attitude among the characters does not exceed the usual Anglican. Religion is important to Jessica Calderon in *Elders and Betters*; it is her children Julius and Dora who parody it in their remarkable worship of their God Chung and his son Sung-Li. Julia Challoner in the late novel *A Heritage and its History* is a devout woman. And there are other such women. It is worth noting that there are more women than men who maintain the traditional belief. It is the case today. Perhaps it has always been. The servants' hall is more religious than above stairs, as we see in *Manservant and Maidservant* and *Darkness and Day*, though the piety finds expression more in hymns than in conduct.

The composition of the novels, covering nearly forty years, would lead us to expect that religion as a feature of family life would be more stressed in the early novels than in the late ones, as is the case. Whatever else we can judge of what has happened in the last forty years, the fact of the further decline of our grandparents' beliefs is inescapable; and the progression of the novels reveals the gradually lessening concern which traditional religion has generally evoked. Of new beliefs or of new forms and ways of faith the novels do not speak. The early concern with religion is shown by the title of the first (post-*Dolores*) novel, *Pastors and Masters*. Here is a conversation among some of the sophisticated people of that work:

> "Are we going to be broad and wicked?" said Emily. "I like that, because I am not very educated, and so still young in my mind. Really, it would be nice to have some religion, and not go on without ever any comfort. And I am not like Nicholas, who is really God's equal, and not his child at all. I think it is better not to have God than to be like that with him."
>
> "It is rather empty for him not to be had," said Bumpus. "He always seems to me a pathetic figure, friendless and childless and set up alone in a miserable way."

"Yes, he has a touch of William in him," said Emily. "But you know he isn't childless. We give even our boys more advantages than that. Mrs. Merry gives it to them."

"You can have him childless in these days," said Bumpus. "But if you have him, I like him really. I like him not childless, and grasping and fond of praise. I like the human and family interest."

"Yes, he tends to be neutral nowadays," said Masson. "Perhaps I do resemble him in that."

"And he had such a personality," said Emily. "Such a superior, vindictive and over-indulgent one. He is one of the best drawn characters in fiction."

"I really cannot listen to this," said Herrick.

Early in the following novel, *Brothers and Sisters*, we are told of Andrew Stace:

> When he spoke of his Maker, he spoke simply of the being who had made him—and perhaps been pleased in this case to execute one of his outstanding pieces of work.

The irreverent tone is typical. But it can become stronger. Here are two of the Ponsonby daughters in *Daughters and Sons*, the young Muriel and her elder sister France, speaking of their aunt Hetta:

> "She goes to church," said Muriel. "And she does not have to go, does she?"
>
> "If she were religious, she would not go," said France. "She would have thought about her religion and lost it."

Elsewhere in this book, when Edith Hallam has been hired as Muriel's governess, this exchange takes place:

> "You do not mind reading the Bible with Muriel?" said Hetta. "I am afraid that is part of the duty you undertake."
>
> "No, not at all, if you don't mind her reading it. I think it is an unsuitable book for a child, but I like it very much myself. I am glad she is to adapt herself to me, and it is good for children to read unsuitable books."

One does indeed feel of the author that at an early age she "thought about her religion and lost it." The attitude can become almost playful as in the names of the Cranmer family in *Parents and Children*: Paul Cranmer, Hope Cranmer, Faith Cranmer, Ridley Cranmer.

Once again, the human is all. No divine framework of events, no supreme arbiter of right and wrong, is admitted. The religious is an escape from the truthful.

Reference to personal mortality is often met with flat humorous denial. Joanna Egerton in *A God and his Gifts* says of someone:

> "You don't mean that she will die? . . . You know she will not. You must know no one will, who is here."

An extended discussion of religion and death and immortality is found in *The Present and the Past*, where the devoted brother and sister Elton and Ursula Scrope are speaking:

> "Don't you take any interest in household things? I take so much."
>
> "I want to have a soul above them, and to be thought to have one."
>
> "I have a soul just on their level. Do you think we have souls?"
>
> "No," said Ursula.
>
> "Do you mind that?"
>
> "Not yet; I am only thirty-two; but when I am older I shall mind it; when extinction is imminent. Now it is too far away."
>
> "We may die at any moment."
>
> "Not you and I. It is other people who may die young."
>
> "Why should we be exceptions?"
>
> "I don't know. I wonder what the reasons are?"
>
> "You don't think you and I will have an eternity together?"
>
> "No, but we shall have until we are seventy. And there is no difference."
>
> "Can you bear not to have the real thing?"
>
> "No," said his sister.
>
> "Then when you are older, will you begin to have beliefs?"
>
> "No, I shall realise the hopelessness of things. I shall meet it face to face."
>
> "And will you be proud of doing that?"
>
> "Well, think how few people can do it. And I must have some compensation; it will not be much."
>
> "I shall not be able to face it. I shall begin to say we cannot be quite sure."
>
> "And I shall like to hear you say it. Even a spurious comfort is better than nothing."

The most explicit statement about what happens after death is made by the dying Sir Ransom Chace in *Darkness and Day*: "I believe I shall be as I was before I was born."

Death is the one fact. Deaths occur in all but three or four of the novels, and since death is the central truth all those who search for truth sooner or later speak of it. "I forgive Nature nothing," says

Terence Calderon in *Elders and Betters.* "Least of all our death at last from natural causes." Another sophisticate in the same novel is Terence's cousin and friend Bernard Donne, to whom the housekeeper Jenney says,

"Money never comes, except from a death, does it?"

"Perhaps that accounts for the sinister touch about it," said Bernard. "It is really death that is the root of all evil. I have always thought it was."

Of the early, middle, and late novels, it is inevitably the late novels that are most occupied with death. Eliza Mowbray says to her son Malcolm in *A Father and his Fate*:

"Life is a strange thing."

"It is death that makes it so," said Malcolm. "Without it life would be well enough."

In *A Heritage and its History*, Julia Challoner is speaking to the butler Deakin:

"Perhaps you should have married, Deakin."

"No, ma'am. There is no end but one."

"You know I do not see it as the end."

"No, you are prepared to go on, ma'am."

"Do you not feel it a happier belief?"

"That hardly bears on it, ma'am. Choice does not play much part."

"So you do not look beyond your death?"

"I have imagined feeling it was all over at last, ma'am. It would seem a sort of compensation. But that is not a thing to expect."

Gaunt Lovat says to his mother Selina in *Darkness and Day*:

"You may not die for a good many years."

"I feel that I may not die at all. Death seems the wrong ending to life. It seems to have so little to do with it."

"You and Chace talk as if you ought to be exceptions to the laws of nature."

"Well, it does seem odd that there should be none," said his mother.

In the early novels the references are less grim, though nearly as persistent. For one example only, here is Nance Edgeworth near the end of *A House and its Head*:

"How difficult it would be, if people did not die! Think of the numbers who die, and all the good that is done! They never seem to die, without doing something for someone. No wonder they hate so to do it, and plan to be immortal."

Endless variations are rung on the theme throughout Miss Compton-Burnett's novels. She is an author born with the notion of mortality. And it has grown. The last truth is found in that last darkness.

III

THE CYNICAL

If the accepted definition of a cynic is Webster's, "one who believes that human conduct is motivated wholly by self-interest," then the word can be applied to the philosophic position of the author of these novels. The word *cynic* implies more of the philosophic than does the adjective *cynical*, which has come to mean, as Webster says, "morose or sneering or sarcastic." The novels are not cynical—their tone is none of these adjectives—but they are the work of a cynic. One searches them for actions not motivated by self-interest, and one finds Maria Shelley, in *Two Worlds and Their Ways*, stealing an ear-ring so that her husband may buy the piece of land he wants; Dudley Gaveston, in *A Family and a Fortune*, remarkably generous with his inheritance; Emma Greatheart, in *Mother and Son*, welcoming home Hester Wolsey, after Hester has behaved so badly to her and to everyone; and there are others: enough to give the events verisimilitude. But for each one of them there are numerous examples of the opposite—for each charity, a dozen meannesses, for each kindness, a dozen cruelties. The reviewer of *The Mighty and Their Fall* in *The Times Literary Supplement*, with whom we have disagreed before, says that "The forces of good and evil are displayed without sentimentality in true balance: there is no cynicism."[3] In fact, there is little else. It is, I suppose, impossible to remove the pejorative connotations of the word *cynicism* and to regard it impersonally, as a philosophic mode; the word *cynical*, and all it suggests of personality, is too close to it.

The novels themselves explicitly support the doctrine. In the following examples, all the speakers are those who have been named the truth-seeking or sophisticate type. They are *good* people. Their voices are the most distinctively appealing among the characters, and closest to the author's own voice. First, here is Dudley Gaveston, cited in the preceding paragraph for his lavish generosity:

"Well, of course, people are only human," said Dudley to his brother, as they walked to the house behind the women. "But it really does not seem much for them to be."

Here are two words from the aged Sir Ransom Chace, the wisest character in *Darkness and Day*. His good friend Gaunt Lovat speaks first:

"There is nothing base in doing and saying what is natural. Unless all nature is base."

"Well, think," said Sir Ransom.

Next, Emma Greatheart, benevolent as her name, in *Mother and Son*:

"Cynicism is never wasted, like efforts or pity."

And, in the late novel *A Heritage and its History*, two examples. The first is from the young Ralph Challoner:

"Cynicism cannot go too far."

A longer discussion among the two sisters Rhoda and Fanny Graham and Julia Challoner:

"It sounds as if you had no good qualities," said Rhoda. "Or as if no qualities were good."

"Those that incur penetration seldom are. If they were, they would not invite it."

"This is cynical talk," said Julia, smiling.

"I am glad," said Fanny. "I tried to make it so."

"Why do you like to be cynical?" said her sister. "Why not choose some other quality?"

"Because cynicism seems clever. And I think it often is."

"Why do we want to be clever?"

"Oh, I think we must want that. And I think we ought. It is good for other people, better than for ourselves."

The cleverness of cynicism may be "good for other people," but it is like a bitter medicine to which some pleasant flavour has been added. One still tastes the bitterness, and knows that it is medicine. It takes a hardy reader to face unflinchingly such a battery of home truths as the Ransom Chaces and the Emma Greathearts send forth. It is a vision of life the severer because it is becomingly dressed out in wit and comedy and humour. One can settle for the cosiness of lesser writers, and the comfort they offer has its traditional values —all art has an element of escape; or for the diversity of greater.

And I do not wish to try to make it sound a brave deed to read and understand Miss Compton-Burnett's novels—the attempt would deserve the laughter of her characters; but the harshness and negativism are there, and to deny them is to deny the whole course of events in the novels, the content and the implications of the dialogue, the extraordinarily authentic fidelity to life which every page reveals.

It is more palatable to take the novels as pessimistic than cynical. Pessimism, to me, however, always suggests the possibility that good fortune and virtue can exist, though we are justified in expecting the opposite. It has the effect of hopes disappointed; yet they were, and perhaps still are, hopes. With cynicism the good fortune (and the noble, the self-sacrificing, etc., etc.) is more than doubted. Thus cynicism is an advanced pessimism or a sub-variety of it. The Greek chorus of the *Agamemnon*, with their "Cry sorrow, sorrow, yet let good prevail!", are pessimistic, not cynical. The cynic believes that good will not prevail, and scants or precludes even the possibility of its doing so.

And pessimism is a broader term than cynicism. Pessimism says that life is dark, while cynicism says that man's actions are predictably base. There is pure pessimism in the novels here and there. They make this kind of wide comment, in the person of Ellen Mowbray in *A Father and his Fate*:

> "Few of us would live at all, if we could foresee our whole future. . . . There are things beyond bearing in every life. We cannot escape them."

Elton Scrope in *The Present and the Past* describes life:

> "It is not short and will not soon be gone. It is longer than anyone can realise. And it is very brave to end it. To say it is cowardly is absurd. It is only said by people who would not dare to do it."

There, if anywhere, are the truly Greek moments in the novels. They sound the heroic notes. They are not common.

Murder is not punished, deceit and falsehood emerge victorious. The *status quo* is preserved. Here are the eldest and youngest Mowbray daughters, Ursula and Audrey, reacting to a dire family event in *A Father and his Fate*:

> "Will things go on in the same way?" said Audrey.
>
> "Yes, people will eat and drink as usual. And, what is worse, we shall do the same. And, worse still, they will know that we do. And, worst of

all, they will soon say we are quite ourselves again. Well, we can say they are quite *them*selves."

What morality, then, is useful? In the last novel, *A God and his Gifts*, the hero Hereward's son and mother discuss moral standards when one of the various paternities of Hereward is brought to light:

> "It is for us to judge this," said Reuben. "There must be some moral standard in human life."
>
> "Standards seem to be based on the likelihood of their being violated," said Joanna.

The one ethical standard which seems absolute, as the discussion in Chapter III of secrets and the search for truth has suggested, is intelligence.

> "But stupidity pushed to a certain point *is*, you know, immorality. Just so what is morality but high intelligence?"

The speaker is Fanny Assingham, in Henry James' *The Golden Bowl*. That the most intelligent people in Miss Compton-Burnett's novels are not the people who are in the positions of power, makes its own comment. But there is another kind of power, the power of observation and comprehension. To see and interpret life, with whatever results of pessimism, is the better kind. It is this vision and this understanding that the novels invite us to share.

CHAPTER SIX

THE NOVELS ONE BY ONE

INTERVIEWER: How do you respond to the feeling of some critics that you have steadily progressed as a novelist, constantly extending the scope and richness of your work?

MISS COMPTON-BURNETT: I don't think I should have thought I had progressed much, on the whole.[1]

I

GENERAL

In the first chapter we have discussed some of the reasons that may account for the lack of marked development or change or progress in the eighteen novels from *Pastors and Masters* to *A God and his Gifts.* In this the last chapter, the main purpose of which is to present a summary of each of the eighteen emphasizing the characterization and special flavour of each, we should at the beginning consider what small changes there have been, no matter how uniform an appearance the novels would as a series seem to present. Simply in any writer's work there are bound to be changes because life is change and his life changes; and the time of composition of these novels covers forty years.

On the lack of thematic development, Angus Wilson has made a very considerable criticism:

> . . . She presents us with a whole view of life and conveys that whole view in a subtle and convincing way, but she does not tell us more of it or show it to us from another side, or make us feel or think about it more deeply than she did from the very start. It is thus, I think, that her work misses greatness, but misses it probably so narrowly that we are constantly urged to set her novels beside the masterpieces of the past.[2]

If the view of life is a whole view of life from the beginning, why want a different or another wholeness? It is inconceivable: but if *Lear* were Shakespeare's only play, would it be less than *Lear* because it was unique? Mr. Wilson, I believe, thinks of the authors—most of them it is—whose works grow, whose *œuvre* we see as an organic whole, whose career and whose art have a shape and pattern and a beginning, middle, and end. *Pastors and Masters* is in many ways tentative, *A God and his Gifts* is in some ways valedictory; but how much more alike they are than *Desperate Remedies* is like *Jude the Obscure*. The view of life has remained more steadily negative even than Hardy's.

In the course of the comments made upon the novels in earlier chapters, a few incidental examples of the developments in character, plot, etc.—what development there has been—have been given, and will be repeated briefly now. A few more will be added. It is convenient to divide the novels into three groups—the early novels, from *Pastors and Masters* (1925) to *Parents and Children* (1941); the middle novels, from *Elders and Betters* (1944) to *Darkness and Day* (1951); and the late novels, from *The Present and the Past* (1953) to *A God and his Gifts* (1963).

The early novels are more interested in religion than in money; money becomes increasingly important in the later novels and finally is identified with power. Some characters, not always the minor ones, are conceived as purely comic types in the early novels, and there is a tendency, though by no means a habit, to divide people into good people and bad people. Comedy of character and wit in general are broader, and events less submerged than will be the case later. The proportion of dialogue to author's-own-comment quite steadily increases; in the early novels the author has not yet effaced herself. In these earlier works there are more descriptions of events, more non-dialogue psychological analysis, far more adverbs and adverbial phrases accompanying the "he-said's" and "she-said's." A page of one of these early novels *looks* more like a page of someone else's novel. The successive pages of pure dialogue come later.

What makes the early novels most obviously early, however, is, though it is obvious, impossible to name. They sound early. They may not bear the customary signs of literary immaturity like ill-defined characters, or padding where there should have been pruning: but they are not immature, they are early. They have, somehow, a clearer tone, a less complex questioning of experience, and a quality of asseveration or self-sureness or emphasis. I do not mean that the later works become ambiguous or faltering. But generally speaking, they are graver works.

In the middle novels there is an overall expansiveness. Scenes, chapters, the novels themselves are longer. They are richer, they have more body. Exposition, scene transition, and grasp of character are so assured that the technical signs of them disappear. Though there is less pure comedy of character, there is more joy. Art is joy, as Yeats said: and each of the four novels from *Elders and Betters* to *Darkness and Day* is a triumph of an author's gifts fully achieved and employed.

The psychology of characters is more complex. To take two examples from *Darkness and Day*: curiosity, in an earlier work, would have been enough (with its attendant traits) to create a character, but the curiosity of Gaunt Lovat is only one aspect of him. The officiousness of Mildred Hallam might have occupied a whole character in an earlier novel, but there is much more to Mildred than this. Gaunt and Mildred have in common that they are good people, even though he is so determinedly prying and she is so aggressively meddlesome.

There are now few of the "type" characters, the fools or fakes or hypocrites. One begins to hear the tone of the sophisticate, who was once a personage in himself, in other characters. The type of the sophisticate spreads and diffuses, though the tyrant remains the tyrant.

The glory of the middle novels is the sustained high comedy of passage after passage. No other novelist or playwright can approach it; it is the supreme dialogue of wit in English.

I can believe that many readers would prefer the late novels to either the middle or early novels. There is something particularly modern in their austerity and economy, something related to the tone of the existentialists, to the novels and plays of Beckett. They are in themselves a concrete music.

They are shorter; sometimes, for the number of characters and the succession of events, too short. Events are often precipitate, and there are big breaks between chapters. There are fewer if any dramatic scenes—the texture is smoother, less variable, seldom if ever articulated into the "set piece" like, in earlier novels, the scene of "thirteen-at-table" in *Elders and Betters* or the scene of Charlotte's accusations against her husband Horace Lamb in *Manservant and Maidservant*. There is a fine arbitrariness to much of the author's method now. For example, the convention of the *sotto voce* remark and the overheard conversation is recklessly employed: two characters while engaged in conversation with a third person, who is presumably standing in front of them, address remarks to one another about him. Which he sometimes hears, but often he doesn't.

Purer and purer as a form, the novels exist by their dialogue, which becomes ever more incisively intelligent and compressed and subtle. The author has disappeared. Dialogue is by now the ultimate value. The old themes are there, but there is less flesh to them; they live more abstractly. There is expert characterization, and even some few comic or humorous people; but the demarcations between characters are less final, either in moral terms or in terms of sophistication, malice, etc. Ortega said in his "Notes on the Novel":

> We want to see the life of the figures in a novel, not to be told it. Any reference, allusion, narration only emphasize the absence of what it alludes to. Things that are there need not be related.
>
> Hence one of the major errors a novelist can commit consists in attempting to define his personages.[3]

The dialogue now carries the entire weight of characterization; we are not told, we "see the life of the figures." The task the author has set herself has become always more difficult; characterization entirely by means of dialogue is a prodigious technical accomplishment.

The scope of the late novels is smaller. The middle novels are like oil paintings; the late are like drawings by Hokusai. Spare and elegant, they suggest as much as they state. But it is the art of statement, crystallized, immaculate, that is their greatest art.

II

THE EARLY NOVELS

Dolores (1911)

Dolores is a Bildungsroman, with undoubtedly a large element of autobiography. It is a curious work, part Victorian, part modern; it clearly shows the influence of George Eliot at the same time it adumbrates the mature style of Compton-Burnett; and it is, in any terms, quite a poor novel—in its difficulties with plot, which lurches forward uneasily among long, uninteresting and static conversations, in its tendency to defeat characterization by over-characterization, and in its troubling switch in point of view, from that of the heroine Dolores in the first two-thirds of the novel to that of her rival and friend Perdita in the last third.

The influence of George Eliot can be seen behind both young women. Dolores, much like Dorothea Brooke in *Middlemarch*, sacrifices herself repeatedly, sacrifices which, with an Eliot-like irony, have their own reward but no other, while Perdita is a little like the charming lightbrained Hetty Sorrel in *Adam Bede*, though a much more morally conscious creature. Dolores' devotion to the scholar preposterously named Sigismund Claverhouse resembles Dorothea's devotion to the Reverend Mr. Casaubon, that austere figure engaged in a "compendium of all the mythologies." The interest in religion, in particular Methodism, is reminiscent of George Eliot. And the theme of the novel, duty, is an Eliot theme.

Very Victorian are such constant addresses to the reader as the following, which indeed sounds an odd note for a novel written in 1911:

> As you watch her, do you mark the something of tone and gesture which touches some familiar chord—such a chord as is touched when, after the remembrance of your friend is dim, you come upon his son grown to a similar manhood?

Although the novel essays a Victorian scope, the texture is thin for the number of years its events occupy; and it markedly lacks what James called "solidity of specification" and Mary McCarthy has called "fact."

This deficiency is related to an extraordinary lack of the visual sense, a sense noticeably missing, though no longer felt as a lack, in Miss Compton-Burnett's mature works. There is much else in *Dolores* whose presence or absence we have marked in its successors—for example, the prevalent use of irony may here be a debt to Eliot but in the later works it achieves effects of which Eliot was never capable. An interest in such themes as the power of jealousy and the strength of family ties, especially the brother-sister relationship, is already apparent. There is at least a tendency towards preserving the unity of place, a stratagem which strengthens the later works. Even mimicry and the *sotto voce* comment already appear. A talent for malice is already to be found in certain of the characters. Felicia Murray is a woman who would be at home in the mature books, with her ironical sophistication, gift for paradox, and habit of humorous self-denigration. Even more striking is the figure of the tyrant foreshadowed in the Reverend Mr. Cleveland.

And there is already humour in *Dolores*, despite the number of deaths (the opening scene is a funeral) and despite a frequent solemnity of tone verging on the lugubrious. I do not mean the inadvertent humour of such oddities as Dolores' habit, while she is mulling over her duties, of standing, not sitting—hours on end. I mean the genuine comedy of Felicia Murray and of the word-wars between the two sisters Mrs. Hulton and Mrs. Blackwood.

But despite all these foreshadowings, it would have taken more than the best of critics, it would have taken a seer, to guess that the author of *Dolores* had it in her to write *Manservant and Maidservant.*

Pastors and Masters (1925)

Thirteen years elapsed between the publication of the first and second novels. *Pastors and Masters* is imperfect, like *Dolores*, but not finally so, as *Dolores* is; it can stand in its own right, and, had the author written no more books, it might still be read with, probably, the kind of interest with which one reads Ada Leverson.

What plot there is, is supplied by the manuscript of a book. Nicholas Herrick, the owner of a boys' school, is, at the age of seventy, finally to bring out an original work. His friend, Richard Bumpus, who is sixty, is also finally to bring out a book. The two books turn out to be the same; Herrick has purloined his manuscript from the room of a dying man, Crabbe, thinking it to be Crabbe's work; but this manuscript is that of a long-lost work of Bumpus. Bumpus has pretended his forthcoming work is a recent product. The secret does not quite come out; only Emily, Herrick's half-sister, guesses. If this account of the plot is confusing, so is the novel. The manuscript has almost as baffling a career as do the earrings of *Two Worlds and Their Ways.*

But plot is unimportant. Much more interesting are the characters —as in *Dolores*, there are both a tyrant, Reverend Bentley, and a sophisticate, Emily Herrick. Reverend Henry Bentley is a fine preliminary study of the tyrannical:

> "I have never met a man so unfortunate in his children. Self-conscious, conceited, with the manners of clowns! Sitting there, thinking their society such a benefit, and then the first words they utter to do with themselves! Neither of them taking the trouble to say good morning to me, but speaking fast enough as soon as they wanted to get off to their own pursuits! It is unbelievable."

Emily Herrick, the best thing in the book, is given to that light and ironic and extremely intelligent power of observation which will supply judgment on all the tyrants in all the future novels. Her range of comment is audaciously large. Here is her first appearance in the book:

> "This is a good room to come back to," said Herrick. "That hall and the woman, and poor Merry shuffling up to do his duty! It made me shiver."
>
> "The sight of duty does make one shiver," said Miss Herrick. "The actual doing of it would kill one, I think."

There is much that is Dickensian in this very short work: the locale, a boys' school, makes one think of him, and there are flat character types, like the fusspot Mr. Merry and his penny-pinching Bible-reading wife—Mr. Herrick's assistants in the school—who have an idiosyncratic appeal, though they are not fully realized even as flat characters. The mealy-mouthed hypocrite, Reverend Francis Fletcher, is a Dickens type, though only sketched; he will reach full flower in Dominic Spong in *Men and Wives*.

Authorial comment is insistent in comparison with later works; plot halts; there are unusually forthright and rather personal-sounding attacks on religion. Pamela Hansford Johnson has pointed out that the date of the events is the latest of any novel, as can be determined by the mention of female suffrage.[4] The total effect of *Pastors and Masters* is of a mild and tentative charm. It will take a darker theme, the preoccupations of tragedy itself, for the comedy to be fully released.

Brothers and Sisters (1929)

This is the first entirely achieved and satisfactory novel. What makes it superior to its predecessors is its strong Greek plot, the curse of incest on the Stace family; the characters, who are with few exceptions completely realized, and among whom the principal figure, Sophia Stace, is a remarkable creation; the wit, which coruscates against the dark background of the family history; and the comedy of character, particularly in the wonderfully tactless ninny, Peter Bateman. Despite the turgidity of some melodramatic passages and, in comparison with later novels, an obtrusive quantity of authorial comment, the overall effect is one of full creativity so fortunately employed as to seem almost thoughtless.

It is the deep and dark theme that has released the wit. Greek even to the extent of employing a prologue chapter, the structure of the story is the double revelation of Christian Stace's birth—first, that he is the illegitimate son of a Mrs. Lang, and second, that his wife Sophia's father, Andrew Stace, was his own real, not merely adoptive, parent. There are so many sets of brothers and sisters—Staces, Batemans, Langs, Drydens, Wakes—that we may miss the irony of the title, which is that Christian and Sophia Stace are not only man and wife but are themselves the sixth pair of brothers and sisters.

The living complexity of Sophia Stace, seen from so many sides, seen in her beauty and power, her self-pity and tyranny and love, makes in comparison most other modern heroines—O'Neill's Lavinia or Williams' Blanche DuBois or Albee's Alice—insipid and flat. One never comes to the end of Sophia; she is immediately *there*, in every scene, unpredictable but always recognizable, almost frighteningly felt and seen and understood. Her children, Andrew and Dinah and Robin, for all their brave wit and stoicism, strive in vain against her. Sophia gains no self-knowledge; this is left to her children:

> "Oh, so many things have gone to the spoiling of us," said Andrew. "Our unnatural life, our want of friends, our thraldom to Sophia, in her success, her sorrow, and now her sickness. We can't tell what has or has not worked our undoing."

Among the other brothers and sisters, Julian and Sarah Wake are the most likeable. Julian is an extremely ironical and charming person—not altogether a man, as he says; his sister is his adoring audience. The Batemans, Tilly and Latimer—who are victimized by their parent just as the Staces are—are a pathetic pair, Tilly with her humble and round-eyed hopelessness, Latimer with his weak scorn of his father and his awkward emulation of Julian's serene wit. The Drydens, Edward and Judith, are hypocrites, particularly Edward, who is a clergyman. The Langs, Gilbert and Caroline, are barely sketched, although they have a pleasing candour and good sense.

There is nothing comforting about Sophia as a mother, and her children turn for tenderness to Miss Patmore ("Patty"), her housekeeper/companion, whose mild and harassed subjection to Sophia has for compensation an extraordinary curiosity, which family events stimulate and satisfy. When Andrew and Dinah and Robin are left alone at the end of the novel, parentless and unmarried, there is some consolation in that the faithful Patty will accompany them to their new home in London. It is by characters that we usually judge a novel, and by this standard *Brothers and Sisters* must rank very high. And it also has wit and humour. But the residual impression the novel leaves is one of power—the power of Sophia as a personality, and the power of her will and of her suffering.

Men and Wives (1931)

In *Men and Wives* the mastery of characterization is complete. There are nearly twenty characters, and each one is sharply defined, speaking in his own tone, exemplifying his own attitudes, and acting a role in the plot which both supports and extends his own individuality. Servants, who are to become more important with each succeeding novel, make their first appearance here in the butler Buttermere, who is pontifical, severe, nosy, and snobbish, and like many a later butler, stands resolutely if precariously on his dignity because he is conscious, and is made conscious, that his position in itself commands so little of it. In Camilla Christy we have a unique study of a loose woman, dazzling, charming, and corrupt; and in the elderly Lady Hardisty we have one of the most outrageously witty of all the sophisticates.

She has ample opportunity for her work, of piercing hypocrisy. A veteran foe is Agatha Calkin, whose benevolent maternalism nearly hides the greediest drive towards power. Dominic Spong is another hypocrite, whose platitudes and proprieties do not quite conceal his hard self-interest. Sir Godfrey Haslam, husband to Harriet, the chief figure in the novel, is an innocent sort of self-deluder—vain of his age and appearance; inadequate to the emotional needs of his wife, and quite human enough, in his more troubled times, to recognize it; irresponsible; self-important; shallow in his affections but making much of them.

Harriet Haslam is a study of the maternal power figure equal in interest to Sophia Stace in the preceding novel, *Brothers and Sisters*. But how different they are. Harriet has all the self-knowledge that Sophia lacks, and it drives her into insanity. Her love for her family, for her foolish husband and for her children, all four of whose ambitions are beneath her own high standards for them, is a brooding, desperate love. Her sleeplessness, her irritability, her illness, are burdens which, as if in reminder of the depth of her love, she willingly inflicts upon her family. They are not of her measure, but it is at the hands of Matthew, her eldest son and the child who is most like her, that she meets her death. The scene of her insanity, an uncanny realization of the soft declivities down which her strong mind has eased itself, and the later scene, almost a love scene, when her son administers poison to her, are both superb, perhaps unequalled for their dreadful drama elsewhere in the novels. Harriet is a love tyrant, and she remains a tyrant even after her death; her children fulfil the ambitions she had in her lifetime wished for them, and her husband is prevented by her will from remarrying.

On this note, of Harriet triumphant even after death, the novel firmly concludes. It is one of the best organized of all the novels, both in its parallels and contrasts, such as Harriet's real motherhood versus Agatha Calkin's travesty of the role, and in its even and orderly spacing of events—such as, to follow a minor character, Camilla Christy's series of men: Reverend Ernest Bellamy, more actor than man; Dufferin, a doctor of harsh and unsparing good sense; Matthew, whose reason for the murder of his mother is in part the fear that she will prevent his marriage to Camilla; Sir Godfrey, on whom Camilla plies her winning ways after Harriet's death; and finally Dominic Spong, the man she at last chooses because of his money. Camilla is in a curious way entirely honest: a considerable contrast to her mother, whom one might call a literary fake, with her "sensitivity" and flowery phrases, usually culled from the familiar poets. By their diction we shall know them: there is the simple directness of the honest people, like Harriet or Dufferin or Rachel Hardisty, and there are all the varieties of platitude and insincerity and elaboration which their moral inferiors resort to—Mrs. Christy and Dominic and Agatha Calkin and the rest. The theme of the novel could be said to be self-delusion or hypocrisy. That Harriet will not delude herself, that she will not spare herself or others the truth, is what kills her. People are happier with their lies, but they do not attain Harriet's grandeur. This and other ambiguities of implication make *Men and Wives* one of the most profound psychological studies among the novels.

More Women than Men (1933)

More Women than Men is not so strong a novel as either of the two novels which immediately precede it. The reason is that the author is here less in touch with her deepest interests: *More Women than Men* does not have the central family dominated by a power figure, and the motif of incest is here only the excessive love which Josephine Napier bears for her nephew Gabriel Swift. Because most of the characters are less actually dependent on the central figure Josephine, they behave more independently, and the result is that the closed-in atmosphere, which has served so well to isolate and magnify the force of the events in *Brothers and Sisters* and *Men and Wives*, has given way to a freer, more general locale, both physical and psychological. There is a school rather than a home, a headmistress rather than a family tyrant. Some of the bitter brave edge of the comedy is blunted. Some of the power is dissipated.

Nonetheless it is a brilliant work. All the minutiae of custom and tone in a girls' school, from the standpoint of those who are in charge of it, are more solidly conveyed than in—to name two recent novels whose setting is also a girls' school—*Olivia* or *The Prime of Miss Jean Brodie*. The sexual interests of the people in *More Women than Men* are mainly homosexual, and homosexuality is regarded in the actual way that the educated English regard it—or, perhaps, refrain from regarding it—with some humour, and with calm and detachment: in other words, from the opposite angle of the outraged and puritanical pruriency of the American way, of Burroughs or Rechy or Blechman. There is more sex by suggestion in this novel than there is in the usual sex-by-statement novel written thirty years later. Here are Josephine and her nephew Gabriel:

> "Do you mind if I smoke in your face?" said Gabriel . . .
> "I mind nothing you do, my boy."
> "Even if the pipe burns your cheek?"
> Josephine remained as she was, her eyes meeting the pipe as if in submission to his pleasure. Presently Gabriel started and moved aside, and in a minute later his wife appeared in the door.

Josephine is a woman of active sexuality the outlet for which is chiefly her school but which finds personal object successively in Gabriel, her nephew (she has long since outgrown interest in her defeated husband Simon, although she had cheated him into marrying her); Felix Bacon, who has been her brother Jonathan's lover for twenty years; and finally Maria Rosetti. Gabriel marries, and Josephine is responsible for his young wife's death, but she finds, once Gabriel is free, that her love has transferred itself to Felix. Felix marries Helen Keats, one of Josephine's staff, and Josephine is left to

Maria Rosetti (also a member of Josephine's staff, but later her partner in the school; Maria is the mother of Gabriel by an early illicit affair with Jonathan, and has witnessed Josephine's murder of Gabriel's wife). Josephine is perhaps the worst liar in all the novels; she lies on all levels, but her most frequent falsehoods are the self-glorifying, self-aggrandising type. She has a brisk, hard mind; she has none of the self-doubtings, the human pitiableness, of her predecessor, Harriet Haslam in *Men and Wives*. Her habit of touching people on the shoulder or patting them on the head is a symbol of all her false familiarity; she insists on being treated as a woman, with all a woman's conventional privileges, and then uses these privileges ruthlessly to gain her ends. Nothing changes her, and nothing finally hurts her; she is an entirely egocentric figure, both repellent and fascinating.

Not all the characters are as fully realized as they are in *Men and Wives* (Elizabeth Giffard and her daughter Ruth, the schoolmistress Theodora Luke, and one or two others lack decisive final touches to their portraits), but in two characters the author's gifts for comedy and wit are splendidly employed. Miss Munday, the senior mistress, is one of the funniest people in all the novels. She says so little that it is always a surprise to hear her voice, but what she says is droll and direct; her habit of amused self-assertion is like a parody of Josephine's humourless egomania. She has been quoted earlier, in Chapter IV.

Felix Bacon is the chief wit. Like Julian Wake in *Brothers and Sisters*, he is himself more woman than man, but his wit is sprightlier, even more self-concerned, and often more broadly humorous than Julian's. His friend, the officious Fane, is inquiring about the death of Felix's father, Sir Robert Bacon:

> "I suppose your father did not hold any dogma?" said Fane.
>
> "I should have supposed that he held the dogma of the Church, as he did."
>
> "His religion was of no help to him?"
>
> "None at all. He died," said Felix.

One is grateful that Josephine does not succeed in her drive to ensnare Felix. That she does not, may be a moral point ; it is, once again, only wit that can serve as an effective weapon against tyranny.

A House and its Head (1935)

Duncan Edgeworth, the first full-scale male tyrant, is as stern a figure as can be found in the novels, and exercises his truculent contempt on his wife Ellen, his nephew Grant, and his daughters Nance and Sibyl. Studiously courteous to outsiders and, for a while, to his second wife Alison, he is vigorously aware of his power in his family, and almost recklessly harsh in his employment of it. Yet one admires him. He is upright; he does not lie; and he has very human needs—for sexual satisfaction, and for the companionship of his nephew Grant, whom he does not banish even after Grant seduces Alison. Duncan is not a devious person, and he has an essential magnanimity of spirit; one pictures him as upright in posture, stiff and inflexible. He is not small in any way.

Not many women novelists have been able to create so male a figure as Duncan, and *A House and its Head* is in other ways remarkable for its characters. Although each successive novel depends more on pure dialogue, the characterization becomes fuller, and in *A House and its Head*, creation is lavish. One character, Dulcia Bode, is so exuberantly conceived that, like Falstaff or Shylock, she comes close to wrecking the fabric of the work which contains her. Though unimportant to the plot, she becomes central whenever she appears, and we wait for the appearances with a kind of horrified anticipation. She is the most broadly comic personage in the novels; her speech is total cliché, she is altogether pushy and aggressive, she has a large, airy, fresh, awkward, and obstreperous talent for malice. She is wonderfully hearty, with a superb gift for denying a slander no one has made and a robust habit of speaking the unspeakable:

> "Hurrah!" cried Dulcia, waving a note above her head. "There is a son born to the Edgeworths! If Alison is held—well, not something of a failure, but not the full success as a consort it was hoped, such feeling will be dispelled today."

Her affections are grotesque:

> "Miss Fellowes!" cried Dulcia, bounding after Beatrice; "I am going to do it. I have screwed my courage to the pitch. Turn and rend me if you must; I am going to take the plunge. May I call you by your Christian name? There, it is out!"

There is little defence against Dulcia, although she is universally deplored. She is impervious to her brother Almeric's sour wit, the quiet contempt of the well-bred Florence Smollett, the outspoken rudeness of old Gretchen Jekyll, who has "hate in her heart" and knows how to utter it.

Among other portraits are those of the pious spinsters Beatrice Fellowes and Rosamund Burtenshaw, rivals in their pursuit of the Reverend Oscar Jekyll, another study of an unbelieving clergyman. Less harmless is Duncan's daughter Sibyl, a girl whose soft affections are often insincere, a false, jealous, pretty creature who arranges the murder of Grant and Alison's child and, by the power of her money, forces Grant to remain her husband even when he learns of the murder. Crime pays her well.

The details of this murder and of its discovery are unlikely and sudden, but the basic structure of the novel—Duncan's three marriages—is strong and simple. Despite his tyranny, despite Sibyl's crimes, this is not one of the darkest of the novels. Dulcia alone is enough to make it a comic masterpiece.

Daughters and Sons (1937)

Although Sabine Ponsonby is one of the most aggressive tyrants of all, her eighty-five years having developed in her a sinister expertise, and although Hetta Ponsonby, her daughter in every sense, is even more implacable as a power figure because her power drive meets with such opposition from her nieces and nephews, *Daughters and Sons* is one of the lightest and most comic of the novels. Although the climax of the novel is the most disastrous dinner party ever given, with Sabine dying during the course of it and Hetta in a ferocious tirade revealing all the family secrets to all the family and their assembled friends, even the dinner party keeps dissolving in laughter. The author is here viewing human foibles with what seems an amused and bemused detachment, and the novel has an unusually large number of sophisticates, whose mocking, intelligent chorus is alert to every event: Stephen Marcon and his grotesque sister Charity, Rowland Seymour, Edith Hallam, who can best Hetta in a word duel, and four of the Ponsonby children—Clare, France, Chilton, and Victor. When their grandmother hisses at them, when their aunt scorns and abuses them, they fight back, led by Clare, the eldest, with an almost abandoned energy.

The fifth Ponsonby child is Muriel. Muriel is much younger, and speaks most of the time in questions—a droll, sensitive child who goes from governess to governess, from family crisis to family crisis, from laughter to tears, with fluctuating comprehension. Muriel supplies the broader comedy, along with two other people—her first governess, Miss Bunyan, whose appetite for food and self-flattery is too robust for Sabine's parsimonious household, and Miss Bunyan's uncle, the Reverend Dr. Chaucer, an unctuous, cliché-ridden, and pompous divine.

Dr. Chaucer is determined upon marriage, and his three proposals of marriage supply a structure to the events—first to Edith Hallam, who marries instead the father in the Ponsonby household, the hardworking and hardpressed writer John Ponsonby; second to another of Muriel's governesses, the terse and composed Miss Blake, who also refuses him; and third to Hetta, who accepts him. The acceptance is grandly ironic—Hetta, who has tried to sweep all before her, who has tried to prevent her brother's marriage to Edith, who has pretended a suicide so that the family will "learn the lesson" of their dependence on her, and thereby caused her mother Sabine such anguish that Sabine declines into senility and death—Hetta ends by accepting the cast-off of two governesses. She is a study of a tyrant in a power position who loses the position. Something or much can be forgiven her, because of her love for her brother, just as much can be forgiven the elder tyrant her mother, who also has a large capacity for love, particularly love of her daughter Hetta, who is the one of her descendants most like herself.

At the end of the novel, Miss Bunyan is to return as Muriel's governess, and we have the sense of a cycle completed. But there have been changes: Sabine Ponsonby is dead and her daughter Hetta and granddaughter Clare are both to be married.

> "What do you think of the changes, Stephen?" said Evelyn.
> "I think but poorly of them. The change for Mrs. Ponsonby is the best. . . ."

There is a coda to these events, a last chapter which concerns Sabine's will. The tutor of Victor and Chilton, Alfred Marcon, who is Sabine's close companion during her last days, mistakenly believes that Sabine has left her large fortune to him. The attempt of the surviving Ponsonby's to persuade him to give it up, and the meanness and malice of Alfred's character, which we have long suspected under his winning ways, are amply revealed in his refusal. Then it is discovered that Sabine has left him only a legacy, the bulk of her fortune going to her family, as all of them have believed it should.

This final example of selfishness may be related to the other larger examples or to the overriding importance of money in this novel or it may be a sign of how tyranny can persist even after death; or it may seem merely tacked on.

The novel is psychologically rich in many ways, such as the jealousy of John Ponsonby, who is a kind man, of his daughter France's writings, or the wonderfully observed spectacle of the fall of Sabine into senility and death. Dire events; but "the worst returns to laughter."

A Family and a Fortune (1939)

This book is all about money. Dudley Gaveston's inheritance of a fortune is used by the family of his brother Edgar as the signal for a display of the acquisitory instinct which is the more remarkable for the disguise it adopts, of doing Dudley a favour by relieving him of his money. The variations on the theme of "true generosity is in receiving, not giving" are pursued *ad infinitem*. The pattern of the novel is provided by Dudley's accession to the fortune, his granting much of it to his family and friends, his withdrawal of these donations when he wishes to marry Maria Sloane, his bitter withdrawal from the scene altogether when Maria decides to marry his brother Edgar, and then his inevitable return to the family, after he has been sick unto death, and the restoration of the original bequests and of the *status quo*. His nephew Clement has consciously engineered the marriage of Maria to Edgar, in the hope that the family will keep all the allowances Dudley has made to them. And it is Clement, a sour and even vicious young man, in whom the worst effects of avarice are conspicuously displayed; Clement becomes a miser, counting his stacks of gold pieces and gloating over them.

The cover of the Penguin edition (1962) of *A Family and a Fortune* rightly describes it as the author's "kindliest" work. Despite Clement, and despite the frustrated venom of an invalid aunt, Matty Seaton, the prevalent tone is cheerful. Edgar's daughter Justine, who is an energetic and officious young woman who never fails to comment where comment would be needless, is yet a good person, strong in her hope for the right, and a capable opponent of her aunt. Even Matty is not without her deeper and better side. Dudley's gentle goodness and the love he and his brother, the hesitant but strong Edgar, bear each other; the figure of Edgar's first wife Blanche, an indecisive and amiable figure who has something of her sister Matty's will to dominate, a rare tyrannical edge to her voice; the touching portrayal of Miss Griffin, Matty's companion and victim—all this creates the kindly tone. Clement, the worst of the Gavestons, is only a minor character; and, more importantly, Matty cannot quite be a tyrant, though she has all the potentialities, because she is not in a position of power. This novel is thus particularly interesting in comparison with the other works; Matty is the only major study of the tyrant *manqué*.

Because a vital and powerful central figure is missing and because there is no other figure of primary stature, the story may not have quite the compelling interest of some of the other novels. The plot is not sensational, and some of the scenes have a certain looseness and leisure to them, but the delirium and death of Blanche and the grave illness of Dudley are two fine scenes. Illness and death often arouse the author's best powers. There is no slackening of the author's energy here, but one feels that the universe is milder. The observation of people is as minutely objective as ever, as can be seen on any page. For one example, here is a brief description of Dudley, exiling himself in pain from his beloved brother's house and fleeing through the snow with Miss Griffin, who has been cruelly thrust forth by Matty:

> Dudley put his arm about her and walked on, leading her with him. She went without a word, taking her only course and trusting to his aid. Her short, quick, unequal steps, the steps of someone used to being on her feet, but not to walking out of doors, made no attempt to keep time or pace, and he saw with a pang how she might try the nerves of anyone in daily contact. The pang seemed to drive him forward as if in defiance of its warning.

Parents and Children (1941)

As if to compensate for the lack of a leading and powerful figure, *Parents and Children* has a wealth of other characters. The nine offspring of Fulbert and Eleanor Sullivan fall into the expected three groups: the young adults—Luce, Daniel, and Graham; the schoolroom trio—Isabel, Venice, and James; and the three youngest—Honor, Gavin, and Nevill. Each of the nine is pictured with complete clarity. Nevill is the most delightful, an infant of three who speaks of himself in the third person and has other dramatic and autocratic ways. One waits for his every appearance. The older eight children are variously intelligent and shy, perceptive and brusque and candid. Hatton, a wise nurse, is the power of the nursery, and commands much more love than the children's mother Eleanor; Mullet, the assistant nursemaid, is one of the supreme comic creations in the novels, with her delusions of past grandeur and her fanciful accounts of it (one is given at the end of Chapter IV)—which the children's scepticism does not prevent their enjoying; Miss Mitford, a tough, resilient, sympathetic, taciturn, selfish woman, is the power of the schoolroom. Another governess, Miss Pilbeam, is as insincere as Miss Mitford is forthright, a quality which invites and is equal to her charges' spirited contempt for her. The various worlds of childhood are seen with a realistic detail of observation which everywhere surprises and at once convinces. After finishing the novel, one can say what the relationship of each child to his eight brothers and sisters is.

And to his elders. Eleanor Sullivan is physically productive as a mother, but psychologically barren. She does not understand a single one of her nine children, and her visits to the schoolroom and nursery are triumphs of incomprehension. The children scarcely tolerate her, if that, in their preference for Hatton and Miss Mitford; and when their father Fulbert is presumed dead in America, they welcome her marriage to Ridley Cranmer as a means of escaping her querulous visitations. Fulbert, in the way of those who leave, inevitably returns; Ridley has suppressed Fulbert's letter which contradicts the earlier report of his death. The beautifully prepared-for and extended scene of Fulbert's homecoming is one of the deeply felt episodes among the novels. Fulbert's gifts for parenthood, although his traces of unctuous self-importance make him less than totally admirable, are as diverse as his wife's are meagre, the reasons being that he differentiates among his children, has a characteristic manner with each of them, and can see their standards as well as his own.

The novel offers what amounts to a metaphysic of parenthood. Regan, Fulbert's mother and the grandmother of the children, has her sense of family in the blood itself, in contrast to Eleanor's nervous preoccupation—which has its own contrast in Eleanor's occasional dry cynical wit. Their neighbour, the caustic and outspoken Hope Cranmer, has no children of her own, only the two stepchildren she does not like, Faith and Ridley; her conversation constantly refers to motherhood and its meaning. Paternity as well as maternity is studied: Ridley seems bent on marriage as much in order to acquire Eleanor's family as to acquire her, and Sir Jesse Sullivan, the husband of Regan and grandfather of the nine children, has an older set of children, the three charming, intellectual Marlowes—Priscilla, Lester, and Susan—who dwell humbly in a cottage at his gates. Their mother was a woman whom Sir Jesse had loved and had not married in South America in his youth. The secret of their parentage, in the way of secrets, is brought to partial light, although Sir Jesse never acknowledges them as his own; but his care for and love of them are seen through his aged taciturnity.

The number of characters and the length of the novel—one of the longest among the eighteen—give it unusual scope. Ridley is a return to the cliché-speaking self-seeker studied in the early novels ("And to the end of my power did I fulfil that trust," said Ridley, in a suddenly full tone. "If feelings arose to the overthrow of a simple spirit of duty, I was helpless as a man and a friend. The emotions of manhood carried me away. I regret if my words are crude; I have no others"). His hypocrisy is thrown in relief by the blunt candour of the younger children. His sister Faith recalls the emptily pious of the earlier novels, though she is less broadly conceived, and not so much comic as chilling in her bland quiet false humility.

III

THE MIDDLE NOVELS

Elders and Betters (1944)

Either *Elders and Betters* or *Parents and Children* is the first of the novels of the major middle phase. One difference between them and the earlier works is that the psychology is more integrated: the characters are less easily divided into the good and the bad. We now realize more fully the implications of Miss Compton-Burnett's remark in her *Orion* conversation with Margaret Jourdain of 1945: "I think it would go ill with many of us, if we were faced by a strong temptation, and I suspect that with some of us it does go ill." It is a kind of moral relativism.

People are both good and bad. For example, the invalid Sukey Donne in this novel, like Matty Seaton in *A Family and a Fortune*, makes her illness an intimidating demand for attention and pity, but the sweetness and beauty of her nature are seen, if rarely, almost as strongly; while Matty is seldom more than a monster. Sukey's sister Jessica Calderon is driven to suicide by her niece Anna Donne, who has accused her, with at least a little justice, of creating a baleful, dark atmosphere in her family. In her too-intense, too-perplexed love for her family, Jessica might recall Harriet Haslam of *Men and Wives*; but Jessica is a pure spirit, almost impersonal in her love, introspective, humble, and principled. Anna herself might seem an embodiment of the brutal and unbeautiful, yet there are admirable features to Anna if one searches for them—her devotion to her family, which is not always merely proprietary, her frankness, which is often honest or struggling to be so, her love for her cousin Terence, which seems sincere. Anna tells a great many lies, but she is true to herself and her aims; more than purely egocentric, she is so enormously devoted to herself that we are tempted to share the devotion. What distinguishes this novel from the earlier novels is a more complex view of personality, and what is essentially a less literary conception of character.

The elders, though they are more highstrung, intense, and heroic than their juniors, are by no means betters. Thomas Calderon falls victim to an elderly infatuation for the young Florence Lacy after his wife Jessica's death, but his deeper love for his daughter Tullia breaks up the proposed marriage. Tullia is a more vivid study of the shallow beautiful selfish daughter than Sibyl Edgeworth in *A House and its Head*; at the end she is to marry the thoroughly agreeable and pleasant Bernard Donne, just as Bernard's especial friend, his cousin Terence Calderon, a subtly selfish, effete, and likeable young man, is to marry the predatory Anna. That Anna has destroyed Sukey's will in favour of Jessica's family and preserved one in favour of herself, and that she has driven her other aunt Jessica to her death, are matters which do not become known; and the novel is also unusual in that it ends with Anna, the chief character, nearly forgotten, our attention instead being concentrated on the marriage of Thomas Calderon, which will not take place, and the marriage of his daughter Tullia to Anna's brother Bernard, which will. The conclusion of the novel seems not so much the formal ending, of marriage and change and the past forgotten, as irrelevant.

The middle novels are also marked by a fecundity of invention, an ease characteristic of an author totally at home with her subject and craft. The figures of the devoted Ethel and Cook alone would have satisfied the Dickens recipe: Ethel, with her habit of speaking in solemn abstraction, and Cook, with her habit of scarcely speaking at all. There are the Calderon children Julius and Theodora, and their bizarre worship of their gods Chung and Sung-Li, rites which depict the strange superstitious knowledge of childhood. There is Claribel, the Donne cousin, and her featherbrained spinsterish self-assertion. There is the brilliant cynicism of Bernard Donne and his cousin Terence Calderon. Once again, in Jenney, the figure of the very humanly curious and sympathetic housekeeper/companion appears, but not here as a victim, rather as an equal, with her own force and position. There are brilliant set scenes, such as the luncheon party where, because there are thought to be thirteen present, superstition takes over and for what seems to be hours all the thirteen refuse to seat themselves. The exposition in the opening chapters is most expert. There is an unusually broad range of axiomatic comment, particularly from the wise young men Bernard and Terence. The novel ends with two deaths having taken place and three marriages about to; but such events in themselves are less satisfactorily conclusive than the sense we have of having observed a rich human panorama. The novel is occupied with death; from the children to their elders, all speak of it; but the comedy is equal to it, and perhaps is its result.

Manservant and Maidservant (1947)

Manservant and Maidservant is the most brilliant of the novels. It is strongly organized, the characterization is freely conceived and firmly executed, and the wit has an élan that borders on hilarity.

The author here has essayed the unusual subject, for her, of showing a change in a character. When we first meet him, Horace Lamb is the most parsimonious of the tyrants; the particular cold nagging and scolding tone he adopts is unique with him. After he has three times been brought close to death—once because his two elder sons had failed to warn him of a dangerous bridge which lay in the direction of his afternoon walk, once because his footman George, whom he had caught stealing, had removed the Danger sign from the same bridge, and once through illness—Horace is a better man. The change is subtle, and comes and goes before it establishes itself finally, but it is convincing, because from the beginning it has been made clear that Horace's nature is complex. Though a despot, his servants admire him, and his dependent cousin Mortimer, a gentle and witty man, is his chief attachment, and returns in large measure

Horace's friendship. Horace's discovery that his wife Charlotte and Mortimer love each other has the effect of making him kind to his and Charlotte's five children—who, aged thirteen to seven, are young enough to be directly susceptible to kindness and old enough to doubt its continuance. At first his kindness is only a stratagem: he knows that much of Charlotte's motivation in wishing to leave him, more, actually, than her love for Mortimer, is to provide her children with a happier home elsewhere; but if the children are happy with their father, she no longer has such firm grounds. However, owing in part to the five children's loving response to his new benevolence, Horace grows into the role. He backslides into harshness but recovers. He banishes his cousin Mortimer temporarily, but welcomes him when he returns. At the end of this novel alone, do we feel that the future course of the family is to be a happier one. The question of what *will* happen to Horace—will he march into moral daylight or retreat into the shadows of self—provides a tension that makes the narrative cohere admirably.

The plot thus outlined—and, despite the usual amount of coincidence and the turgid passages in which Horace's near-fatal illness is described, the plot is an excellent one—seems even remoter than usual a vehicle for humour. But this novel is very high comedy indeed. There are a verve, sharpness, and elegance to the wit which support the happier outlook—which in turn allows the happier ending to the events.

In America, as published by Knopf, the title to the book was *Bullivant and the Lambs*, and it is in the butler Bullivant that the author's comedy of character reaches its height. Suave, distinguished, pompous, and at the same time humanly curious and aware, with an impish talent for malice, a good heart, and an unequalled command of rhetoric, Bullivant dominates the book. His fellow-servants are worthy of him—Mrs. Selden, the cook, with her serene self-righteousness and her tendency to abandon herself in religious song; George, the workhouse boy with, for a beginning footman, uppity notions and occasionally the courage to do mortal verbal combat with Bullivant; Miriam, the orphanage girl, round and red, who wishes her name was Lily or Rose—all these make the kitchen the warm centre of the novel. It is the tribunal of the above-stairs, and has its own energetic life. As comedy it lacks Dickens' poetry and fantasy, but it is in other ways richer—the characters are less repetitive, and they are fuller, more intelligent, more human and more absurd. To quote is especially an injustice here, since so full a fabric of relationships supports every line of dialogue, but the following short excerpts may afford representative glimpses of the great Bullivant. Here he is at his most magisterial:

> "Miriam," said Bullivant, in a distinct tone, "will you have the goodness to be as expeditious as possible, in order that George may succeed you at the sink? There are matters requiring his attention, when those that claim your own, are disposed of. I am much obliged to you, Miriam."

Or in a philosophic mood:

> "A servant I am, and a servant I remain, George," said Bullivant, in a low, melodious voice, addressing the idea of George and the walls of the kitchen, and glancing to see if Cook were also of the audience. "So it is; so it has been; so it will be; and I am satisfied."

Or, in a conversation with Mortimer Lamb concerning the tutor Gideon Doubleday, with his sense of humour in play:

> "I think he is afraid of his mother."
>
> "Well, sir, that might be said of many of us."
>
> "Were you afraid of yours?"
>
> "I would never open my mouth against her, sir."
>
> "Do you feel that she can hear you?"
>
> "There are things beyond us, sir."
>
> "I suppose she is dead?"
>
> "You are right that she has passed on, sir."
>
> "Do you expect to be reunited?"
>
> "Well, sir, I would not be definite, united perhaps being hardly the word in the first place. But anything derogatory applies only to myself."
>
> "Do you wish you had been a better son?"
>
> "Well, there are things in all our hearts, sir. Not that I ever forgot that she was a woman. It was only that I was confronted with her being other things."
>
> "Will you think of it on your deathbed?"
>
> "That will be rather late in the day, sir."
>
> "It might be thought to be the right moment."
>
> "Well, in that case, sir, it may be put into my mind. But I shall not go to seek it. Making my peace at the last moment is hardly in my line. And my mother would have condemned it. That was hardly her tendency, sir. Indeed the whole thing was that her standard was too high. In one sense I could not have had a 'better' mother." Bullivant ended with a smile and turned towards the kitchen.

Two Worlds and Their Ways (1949)

Two Worlds and Their Ways, one of the seven chapters of which takes place in a girls' school and another in a boys' school, and the novel of 1933, *More Women than Men*, almost all of which is laid in a girls' school, show interesting differences between the author's early novels and those of the middle period. The comedy of the earlier work depends more on the comedy of character (Miss Munday, Mrs. Chattaway, etc.), while the later novel has more of the comedy of wit, is more intellectualized and epigrammatic; *More Women* has a sensationalistic plot, while *Two Worlds* has one of the best-organized plots of all the novels, with marked symmetry to the events, and the events, despite their complexity, proceeding one out of the other in a natural and coherent manner. The closed-in atmosphere of a girls' school is created with a more traditional use of novelistic detail in the first novel, although the second gains from its contrast between the two schools—from the ways girls of around thirteen behave contrasted with those of boys of a slightly junior age. In both schools in *Two Worlds* the details are more suggested than stated. The same is true of homosexuality, which finds a more prominent part in *More Women*, though it is a pervasive if subtle strand of *Two Worlds*. There is no tyrant in the latter novel to compare with Josephine Napier in the earlier; instead, the drive towards power is shown in Lesbia Firebrace, owner of the girls' school, who is more irritating than awful, and in the characters of Sir Roderick Shelley and his wife Maria, whose excessive ambitions for their daughter Clemence and their son Sefton lead both children to embark on a career of cheating at their respective schools, in both cases detected. But Sir Roderick and his wife are not grossly tyrannical; they are ordinary and loving parents, with a power impulse that suits.—It is hard to say which is the better novel. *More Women* is bolder in its outlines but cruder (the word is of course highly relative), while *Two Worlds* has a proficiency and flow to the dialogue which may balance the more robust humour of the early work. It is a matter more of personal preference than absolute standards.

Despite the symmetry—of Clemence and Sefton's cheating, and the subsequent discovery of their parents' "cheating" of another kind (Sir Roderick has fathered an illegitimate child, and his wife Maria has stolen an ear-ring), the plot relies to such a degree on coincidence that it becomes a parody of the device, a *reductio ad absurdum* which has its own value. Maria visits a shop near Sefton's school to sell a stolen ear-ring at the very moment Oliver Spode arrives to sell the other ear-ring for his mother. *Two Worlds* becomes a book about ear-rings. Oliver's mother was the mistress of old Oliver Firebrace long ago, and when their affair had ended (the result of it being the existence of Oliver Spode), he gave her one ear-ring as a gift. It is a very odd gift, one ear-ring. Coincidental too, is that Oliver Spode becomes the lover of Oliver Shelley (there are three Olivers!), who is Sir Roderick's son by his first marriage (and therefore Oliver Firebrace's grandson, Oliver Spode's nephew, and half-brother to Clemence and Sefton). To complicate the family relationships further, Maria steals and sells the ear-ring in order to buy a piece of land for her husband which he had sold from the Shelley estate long since. The reason for the sale had been twofold: Roderick needed the money for his father-in-law (Mr. Firebrace) to give his mistress (Oliver Spode's mother), and he also needed it for himself to give his own mistress (these events occurred before his second marriage, that to Maria), who is the butler Aldom's mother Elizabeth. Elizabeth married, and used her share of the money to buy the same farm; it seems likely that real estate values fluctuated sharply at the time. All this may be too hard to follow, and it is perhaps a critical comment that it is; but at least the moral symmetries emerge: that Maria's transgression, of stealing the ear-ring, is balanced by her husband's early transgression (and restores to him the land sold to pay for that transgression), that old Mr. Firegrace has committed the same transgression as his son-in-law, and so on.

The good angel of these events is Juliet Cassidy, a sophisticate who, as is not usual, takes a leading part in them. She is old Mr. Firebrace's daughter (and also the wife of the owner of the boys' school which Sefton briefly attends and in which Oliver Shelley is briefly engaged as music master), and therefore Sir Roderick's sister-in-law by his first marriage. She buys and returns the ear-ring Maria has stolen and sold, and protects Maria by her kindness and wit. In view of the careers of their elders, the cheating of Clemence and Sefton seems trivial; in the two worlds of home and school, it is the former where misconduct most flourishes.

Darkness and Day (1951)

"The future is to have its sorrow running through it, its questions of the shadow over certain lives, its darkness at the back of the day. We will try not to forget it; that carries the danger of remembrance. But we can try to turn our eyes from it, and keep them to the light."

Edmund Lovat is speaking to his family, early in *Darkness and Day*. Edmund and Bridget have long and mistakenly believed that they are father and daughter as well as husband and wife, a belief which has shadowed most of their married life and made of Bridget a woman of exacerbated sensibility and of their two daughters, Rose and Viola, the most precocious and recalcitrant of children. When the truth is discovered, the damage has been done; one can even sense a certain disappointment in Edmund and Bridget at being robbed of the importance attached to a tragic position. Other, though not all, secrets of the Lovat and Chace families are revealed, but the illumination which ensues is but flickering. The darkness of human error is natural, and it is difficult to walk in the light.

This tone is reinforced by many references to the history of King Oedipus and to the general nature of tragedy. Bridget has the resoluteness and singlemindedness, the intensity, and the powers of self-recognition which Greek tragic heroines have, but she falls short in other respects; she is not big enough, or grand enough, and, most of all, we do not see ourselves in her, her problems are not made significantly ours, her experience is like an example in a textbook rather than immediate, mythic, and final.

The dialogue returns persistently to the subject of death; as is natural, since Sir Ransom Chace, head of one household, is eighty-eight, and Selina Lovat, head of the other, is not much younger. The novel ends with the death of Sir Ransom, and of course with some pages of discussion of it and of his will.

The dialogue, whatever its subject, has become drier—bonier, more skeletal. It requires closer attention: the sentences are shorter, the use of logical ellipsis is more arbitrary, and the wit is subtler and swifter and could not be more terse. The opening pages are the most incisive dialogue in the novel—a sustained display of epigrammatic wisdom by the ancient cynic Sir Ransom. The talk in the servants' hall is, as one would expect, more openly humorous. Its chief effects are derived from the young footman Bartle, who is the soul of impertinence, and whose derisory comments upon his elders—the butler Ambrose, a shade of Bullivant; the severe and proper housemaid Alice; and the robust person of the cook Mrs. Spruce—meet with spirited efforts to repress him and them. A fifth member, a mite of a housemaid named Tabitha ("Tabby"), is an innocent counterpoint to the worldliness of the three elder servants.

Rose and Viola Lovat, aged ten and eight, have their human side: Viola's fear of the dark, their occasional naïveté, their fondness for the maternal Mrs. Spruce and for their grandfather—as he turns out to be—Sir Ransom. But nine-tenths of the time they seem like studies of the girlhood of Goneril and Regan. To their very temporary governess, Mildred Hallam, an officious and positive yet not unlikeable young woman, they are fiends, relentlessly insulting and intractable. There is something pathetic in Mildred's efforts to befriend and instruct them, since she knows, as they do not, that she is their half-sister. Her efforts are defeated. It is a negative novel; its dominant mood is more darkness than day.

IV

THE LATE NOVELS

The Present and the Past (1953)

Darkness and Day is the borderline novel between the works of the middle period and those of the late period. *The Present and the Past* is shorter, although the cast of characters is not fewer, nor is the plot less eventful; the result is that we do not see enough of characters we especially want to, while other characters are sometimes so briefly established that they remain shadowy, and that the actions of the novel follow one another precipitately. Cassius Clare, the hero of *The Present and the Past*, talks of suicide on one page, and five or six pages later has committed it (or pretended to); his first and second wives meet for the first time, and between chapters become fast friends. Restraint becomes austerity, and the psychological processes that in the past were treated in detail tend now to be guessed by their sudden results—e.g. Cassius's pretended suicide. The authority of presentation has in no way lessened; if anything it has increased. But if there is a certain ratio between characters and events, on the one hand, and the quantity of events they occupy, on the other, that strikes us as proportionate in a novel, this ratio has now become a little top-heavy. Always the most economical of writers, Miss Compton-Burnett has become parsimonious.

Cassius is a return to the power figures, and in his alternations of testiness and amiability, of flattery and contempt, is a compelling picture of an unstable man. The past, in the form of his first wife, impinges upon the present, in the form of his second; attracted to both, and disregarded by them in their sudden intimacy, he becomes increasingly isolated, and dies. The tyrant must have his dependants, and keep them that way; his isolation thus *is*, symbolically, his death. Cassius is a study in the tyrant who fails. He is judged or ignored or mocked by his children, his father, his wives; the novel begins with the death of a hen, and ends with his. His friendliest relationship is with his butler Ainger, who, himself a fatuous man, must face the ridicule of the numerous other servants in the kitchen. Just as Ainger lacks the intelligence and poise of earlier butlers like Bullivant or Ambrose, Cassius lacks the mentality of those large-looming people like Sabine Ponsonby or Horace Lamb in the earlier novels. Money is not the problem it is in many of the other works, and this familiar means of exercising sway is denied Cassius. His death is more like extinction.

The rare and delightful gift for fantasy, which has been seen in the Calderon children's religious rites in *Elders and Betters*, reappears here, in the death of a mole, for whom the younger children conduct a burial service. Here is the funeral sermon of Toby, the three-year-old:

> "O dear people, we are gathered together. Dearly beloved brethren. Let us pray. Ashes and ashes. Dust and dust. This our brother. Poor little mole! Until he rise again. Prayers of the congregation. Amen."

Other very attractive figures beside Toby and the mole are the brother and sister Elton and Ursula Scrope, whose lives are devoted to each other and to each other's wit, as well they might be. A surprise in the servants' hall, after the grand foolishness of Mrs. Selden in *Manservant and Maidservant* and the warm and comfortable Mrs. Spruce in *Darkness and Day*, is the cook Mrs. Frost in the present work. She has a private sense of the ridiculous which flashes forth in occasional devastating comments; she is self-amused, cynical, and remote.

Mother and Son (1955)

Mother and Son is a better novel than the one before it, *The Present and the Past*. Because there are fewer characters and the plot is simpler, the texture of the novel is less thin. It is a *locus classicus* of some of the leading themes and motifs of the novels.

Here, all secrets emerge, in the dramatic scene in which Hester Wolsey, who has planned to marry the widower Julius Hume, and has carried out an elaborate campaign to that end, discovers that Julius is to marry Emma Greatheart, with whom Hester had lived for many years before coming to the Hume household; and that his son Roseberry is to marry Emma's housekeeper/companion Miss Burke. Hester's jealousy—an emotion frequently analysed in the novels—is so intense that it becomes a spectacle in itself, and she reveals that the nephews and nieces of Julius are in fact his illegitimate children; that Rosebery is in fact not Julius's son but the illegitimate child of Miranda, Julius's recently deceased wife; and that Rosebery has first offered marriage to her before offering it to Miss Burke, an offer which Hester, her eye on the head of the household, refused. Both contemplated marriages are called off by the women concerned, and Hester leaves her post with the Hume family to return to her friendship with Emma. The pattern of outsiders attempting to merge with the central family is important here. Hester is able to carry out the scene of revelation because she has a genius for overhearing very private conversations. Still another device used here with special emphasis is the *sotto voce* conversation, which is indulged in incessantly by Julius's three children. As for curiosity, we see it in its quintessence in the tutor Mr. Pettigrew; he lives and breathes and has his being in gossip about the Hume household.

The basic theme, however, is Rosebery Hume's attachment, this side idolatry, to his mother Miranda. Miranda is a return to the pure tyrant; although she dies half-way through the novel, her influence persists to the end. Indeed the last words of the novel refer to Rosebery's attachment to his mother, which survives her death, the attraction of other women, and Julius's patient ironies. Rosebery is as heavy in speech as in person; a foolish man, no doubt, with his elaborate devotion to all that is feminine, and not without some womanly touches of his own—yet he is also likeable, in that he is without malice, his manœuvres are always pathetically transparent, his pomp is engagingly innocent. He is most unlike his mother, an old woman of insistent and brutal forthrightness. The following statements are typical of her: "I am alive to all that happens in my house" and "I am not in the habit of pretending" and "There is nothing I cannot say."

The cat Plautus, adored by Emma and Hester, but not by their housekeeper Miss Burke, is as alive as any animal character in literature, and more than most human ones. The natural gifts of an author, the rare ability to see totally and record accurately, are epitomized in the lifelikeness, or cat-likeness, of Plautus. In answer to Miss Burke's question "Who was Plautus in real life?", she is told by the two women friends:

> "He was a Latin writer," said Miss Greatheart. . . . "I think he wrote plays; not very good ones."
> "Why did you call the cat after him?"
> "Well, he has not written any good plays either," said Miss Wolsey, holding out her hand to Plautus, who came and considered it, as if in the hope of finding some offering.

Emma Greatheart, a large woman of sixty, whose manner is vague but whose mind is not, is very pleasant. Her forgiveness of Hester without seeming to forgive her is her kindest act of all. Her sense of nonsense, her playful wisdom, her self-confessed selfishness make her one of the most appealing of all the sophisticates.

A Father and his Fate (1957)

Less fatuous than Cassius Clare in *The Present and the Past*, and not one of the harsh tyrants like Duncan Edgeworth in *A House and its Head*, Miles Mowbray, who is the father of the title, can be both fatuous and harsh. He can play indulgent and foolish Lear-like tricks on his three daughters, and in another mood he can sternly point out their dependence on him for food and shelter. He can be testy and peremptory, affectionate and even loving. Most of all, he is a tyrant who gets what he wants. When his wife Ellen is believed to be lost at sea, he takes his adopted heir's fiancée, Verena Gray, away from him; when he finds out his wife is still alive, he nonetheless proceeds with his plans for his marriage to Verena. Although this is prevented by Ellen's return, and Verena is at last married to her original intended, Malcolm, Miles admits no guilt. Unwilling to play second fiddle to Ellen, Verena leaves Malcolm and the novel; after his divorce, Malcolm marries Ursula, the eldest and best of Miles' three daughters. The secret that Verena's child was fathered by Miles and not by Malcolm is known to only two or three people besides Miles, and they are peripheral characters. So that Miles' fate is happy. He ends with his family about him, with no damage done to his own life—only to others'. Not noble to start with, his fate does not ennoble him. Happy fates do not ennoble.

Every other character in the novel acts like a chorus to comment on Miles' conduct. He is the hub; it is he who acts. Even Eliza Mowbray, the wife of his deceased brother and a tyrant in her own right, exercises no real independence of action; she reacts to Miles' adventures rather than acting on her own. She might seem intended as a contrast or parallel to Miles in that, as he has three daughters, she has three sons (the eldest of whom is Malcolm, Miles' heir), but if the contrast is intended, it is not carried very far. It is an existentialist situation, that Miles alone acts, and names his acts, and from his acts constructs his *ex post facto* codes. There are no young children to share the spotlight in Miles' drama, and only one servant, the snooty butler Everard, appears for a moment or two.

In an earlier novel, the character of Constance, Miles' second daughter, might have been used as a strong contrast, in her piety and righteousness, to her free-thinking sisters and cousins; but as she is here, her voice is no more than an occasional discordant note in their intelligent cynicism. Because Miles is entirely central, the other characters may seem less strongly conceived than characters in other novels. Miles himself is not so interesting as some of the other tyrants. He is completely understood and presented, but he lacks the bravura of temperament typical of some of the other people with power. He is alive, but not so compellingly and importantly alive as some.

A Heritage and its History (1959)

Just as *A Father and his Fate* is organized around Miles Mowbray and his simple egoism, so *A Heritage and its History* centres about Simon Challoner and his love for the family estate. Simon's uncle, Sir Edwin Challoner, is childless, and the love that might have gone to wife and children has gone instead to his brother Hamish, Simon's father, just as Simon's own chief affection has gone to his brother Walter, a clever and perceptive poet. After the death of Hamish, Sir Edwin is so much alone in his life that he marries for companionship, and his new wife Rhoda bears a child to Simon. Marriages or near-marriages of an elderly man and a young woman appear elsewhere in the novels (Duncan Edgeworth in *A House and its Head*, Thomas Calderon in *Elders and Betters*, Miles Mowbray in *A Father and his Fate*). They are never lucky.

Sir Edwin takes the child born to his wife and Simon as his legal heir. His motives are pride and the desire to punish Simon. Simon for many years lives in a nearby house, longing for the heritage of which a moment's pleasure had bereft him. He marries Fanny, Rhoda's sister, and it is when their five children begin to mature and their daughter Naomi wishes to marry Sir Edwin's "son" (named Hamish after Sir Edwin's beloved brother) that the truth is revealed: Naomi is the half-sister of Hamish. The young Hamish at first renounces the heritage in favour of Simon, but soon reclaims it, when he finds a woman to replace Naomi. His marriage to Marcia is short; he dies, childless, of a heart ailment, and the heritage is finally, after many years, returned to Simon, who enters into his own as into a kingdom.

All this sounds like the structure of a family chronicle. But it is a very short novel. Between chapters VI and VII we leap twenty or so years, and between chapters VIII and IX another five years. Events are truncated or abrupt; character interest, except in the case of Simon, is not sustained. For example, Rhoda, Simon's wife, who begins as an interestingly emancipated yet conventional woman, has, by the end, become merely a series of exclamation points. Too many events, too many characters, in too short a space. At the end of the novel one can feel that there are five or six widows floating about (there are three), and although a certain resolution is achieved—Simon has his heritage, and is once again, or perhaps for the first time, a calm man—it has been too much of a rush.

The proportion of dramatic or melodramatic speech is very high. Witty dialogue, when it appears, is sharp and effective, but there is not enough of it. There is not enough of the butler Deakin, "whose look of complete resignation was the key to his character," nor of the infants Emma and Claud. There are too many characters for the reader or the author to retain his grasp of, and one major character, young Hamish's wife Marcia, is introduced near the end—never an advisable literary strategy. The mood is very dark; the creeper that enshrouds the house at the beginning enshrouds it a generation later, at the end; between, there has been ceaseless talk of death, unless talk of old age and of the threat of the workhouse or orphanage intervenes. If one could see or feel the heritage, if one had more the sense of place, the novel which it dominates would have been better. "We have known the place and served it," says Fanny, Simon's wife. "We have seen it regarded as something it could not be. As a force in the background, with human lives helpless in the fore." One can take the comment in this novel as historical; the love of land pictured here has not survived in the same form into the twentieth century. But the other more permanent interest of human beings is in this novel less richly satisfied.

The Mighty and Their Fall (1961)

The irony of the title of this novel is that, though the mighty may fall, they sustain no damage. Ninian Middleton, the head of the family, attempts to destroy one will of his dying brother Ransom, which left Ransom's fortune to his niece, Ninian's daughter Lavinia, in order to preserve an earlier will in favour of himself. The attempt fails, and knowledge of the failure is made public; but Ninian's hard rational aplomb does not for an instant falter. Indeed he takes the offensive, accuses before he is accused, attributes his own motives to a desire for the welfare of his family, and finds in others' motives his own unadmitted selfishness. His reaction to his guilt is a strong contrast to that of his daughter Lavinia, who, in her wish to prevent her father's remarriage, is guilty of temporarily suppressing a letter from Teresa Chilton, who has first accepted, then rejected, and then accepted—in the letter Lavinia hides—Ninian's proposal. Lavinia in her guilt becomes a tormented and driven woman. It is not only the fact that Ninian is much older than his daughter that makes him incapable of remorse at his deed: to the powerful all things naturally accrue, even ease of conscience. The structure of the novel has this strong duality, of two deeds and their consequences; and throughout there flows the constant close attachment of father and daughter. At the end of the events Ninian has gained what he wanted: his wife, most of his dead brother's fortune, the cancellation of his daughter's plans for marriage. He has not learned from the experience: he has not seemed to need to learn.

Money is most important in this novel. Religion is dealt with to its detriment; unbelief is the norm among the characters, and rather insistently proclaimed. There are a sprightly young butler, Ainger, and a sour and repressive cook, his elder. Young children are again prominent in this novel, in the three younger offspring of Ninian, Agnes, Hengist, and Leah. Agnes is an insincere and self-loving girl. Hengist and Leah are dour little rationalists, engaged in daily warfare with their heroic governess Miss Starkie. The wit is tighter and more attractive than in the preceding novel; there is less melodrama. Comedy of character cannot be said to exist. In all, *The*

Mighty and Their Fall is a somewhat better novel than its predecessor in its clean, distinct plot and in its narrower and deeper focus.

A God and his Gifts (1963)

Hereward Egerton is the "god-like spirit" who "creates life and destroys it," as one of his sons says of him. Hereward is a popular novelist, and the lives he has created in fiction "have cheered the homes of thousands," as he himself says. But his private life—none of which remains so, since all secrets are revealed in this novel with extraordinary neatness—is equally creative. His relationship with Rosa Lindsay, his mistress before he marries, does not result in a child, but he is the father of his wife's sister's child and of his son's fiancée's child. He is on his way to seducing the fiancée of another son, but the latter's vigilance intercepts him. Like a god Hereward is beyond morality, and his matings are like the matings of a god with mortals. He has an entirely devoted sister to protect him, he has fame and adulation, he has full consciousness of his powers and he exercises all of them. He is the masculine principle, turned loose in a late-Victorian country house. He is a compelling character, because he is a basic principle believably clothed in human flesh.

Hereward is the apotheosis of the power figure in that his resemblance to the gods is frequently and openly referred to. This is no new theme in the novels—Ninian Middleton in the preceding novel, for example, is identified with God. But there is something impersonal about Hereward—a serenity and sureness beyond the anger and jealousy and emphasis of the earlier God-father-tyrant figures. The difference may be that Hereward is a writer. There have been dozens of writers in the novels, but none before has been the dominating figure that Hereward is. And *A God and his Gifts* is thus an apotheosis novel in another sense: that the writer and writing are the chief subject of the dialogue. Hereward's father regards fiction as a low and easy thing; the butler Galleon believes that writing is beneath a gentleman; and there are all sorts of other attitudes. Hereward himself is grateful to his sister for protecting him from "those arch enemies of the artist, parents and home." What creativity means, in terms of the artist's temperament and tastes, is the subject. Even if extraneous to the value of the novel as such, Miss Compton-Burnett's ideas about the artist and his art, in this her nineteenth novel, are fascinating. Perhaps the present novel is the only one of the nineteen which depends for its greatness on some knowledge of the themes of the earlier works.

But it has its special values. The portrait of Hereward is masterful in a double sense, and every member of a large cast, from Hereward's father Sir Michael, an amiable and innocent old man, down to the infants Henry and Maud, has a distinct tone and individuality. The characters are conceived kindly, even gently, and there are no harsh or violent people among them. The novel is short; breaks between chapters are abrupt; the last chapter is attenuated: but the revelation of Hereward's life and loves provides a large sustaining interest. The dialogue is often at its best, especially in the sophisticated persons of Joanna Egerton, Hereward's mother, and Reuben and Trissie, his son and his son's fiancée. Henry is the best of all the infants, with the possible exception of another three-year-old, little Nevill in *Parents and Children*, and he is given the last line of the novel, which expresses his desire to marry little Maud, who is only two. The marriage would be incestuous, since little Maud is his half-sister. All the old themes are here—incest, power, secrets, and so on—and here are seen with a final clarity, a clarity which has the ultimate compassion, of those who understand and do not judge.

NOTES

CHAPTER I

[1] V. S. Pritchett, "Prospects for the English Novel," *New York Times Book Review*, Apr. 17, 1949, p. 22.

[2] Edgar Johnson, *Charles Dickens, His Tragedy and Triumph* (New York, 1952), I, 304.

[3] The original of this letter, to Richard Best, dated Apr. 9, 1917, is in the National Library of Ireland, in Dublin.

[4] I. Compton-Burnett and M. Jourdain, "A Conversation," *Orion: A Miscellany*, I (1945), 25.

[5] Ibid.

[6] Edward Sackville-West, "Ladies whose bright Pens . . .", chapter VI in *Inclinations* (London, 1949), p. 83.

[7] "Interview with Miss Compton-Burnett," *Review of English Literature*, III (Oct., 1962), 111.

[8] Bernard McCabe, "Ivy Compton-Burnett, An English Eccentric," *Critique* (Univ. of Minnesota), III, no. 2 (1960), 60. On the relationship between Compton-Burnett and Sarraute, see Christine Brooke-Rose, review of *A God and his Gifts* [and of Iris Murdoch's *The Unicorn*], *London Magazine*, n.s. III (Mar., 1964), 83–86. The central statement of Nathalie Sarraute on Miss Compton-Burnett's dialogue is in her essay "Conversation et sous-conversation," in *L'Ère du Soupçon* (Paris, 1956), 123–124:

> Mais le lecteur n'est que rarement tenté de se départir de sa vigilance. Il sait qu'ici chaque mot compte. Les dictons, les citations, les métaphores, les expressions toutes faites ou pompeuses ou pédantes, les platitudes, les vulgarités, les maniérismes, les coq-à-l'âne qui parsèment habilement ces dialogues nc sont pas, comme dans les romans ordinaires, des signes distinctifs que l'auteur épingle sur les caractères des personnages pour les rendre mieux reconnaissables, plus familiers et plus "vivants": ils sont ici, on le sent, ce qu'ils sont dans la réalité: la resultante de mouvements montés des profondeurs, nombreux, emmêlés, que celui qui les perçoit au dehors embrasse en un éclair et qu'il n'a ni le temps ni le moyen de séparer et de nommer.
>
> Sans doute cette méthode se contente-t-elle de faire soupçonner à chaque instant au lecteur l'existence, la complexité et la variété des mouvements intérieurs. Elle ne les lui fait pas connaître comme pourraient y parvenir les techniques qui plongeraient le lecteur dans leur flot et le feraient naviguer parmi leurs courants. Elle a du moins sur ces techniques cette superiorité,

d'avoir pu atteindre d'emblée la perfection. Et par là elle a réussi à porter au dialogue traditionnel le plus rude coup qu'il ait subi jusqu'ici.

CHAPTER II

[1] "Interview with Miss Compton-Burnett," *Review of English Literature*, III (Oct., 1962), 101. Miss Compton-Burnett gave the same description of her work in another interview: Frank Kermode, "The House of Fiction: Interviews with Seven English Novelists," *Partisan Review*, XXX (Spring 1963), 72.

[2] Cecily Mackworth, "Les Romans d'Ivy Compton-Burnett," *Critique* (Paris), XIV (May, 1958), 397.

[3] "An Extra Grudge Against Life," review of *A God and his Gifts*, *Time*, LXXXIII (Feb. 14, 1964), 100.

[4] V. S. Pritchett, "Miss Compton-Burnett," review of Robert Liddell's *The Novels of I. Compton-Burnett*, *New Statesman and Nation*, n.s. XLIX (Mar. 5, 1935), 329.

[5] Robert Liddell, *The Novels of I. Compton-Burnett* (London, 1955), pp. 90–92.

[6] Frank Kermode, review of *The Mighty and Their Fall*, in "Fiction Chronicle," *Partisan Review*, XXIX (Summer, 1962), 471.

[7] Elizabeth Bowen, "Ivy Compton-Burnett," in *Collected Impressions* (New York, 1950), p. 84.

[8] "Aeschylus and Austen," review of *The Mighty and Their Fall*, *The Times Literary Supplement*, Sept. 22, 1961, p. 625.

[9] Trans. Philip Vellacott, Penguin ed. (London, 1959), pp. 71 and 87.

[10] Evelyn Waugh, "Op. XV," review of *A Father and his Fate*, *Spectator*, CXCIX (Aug. 16, 1957), 223.

[11] Angus Wilson, "Ivy Compton-Burnett," review of Robert Liddell's *The Novels of I. Compton-Burnett*, *London Magazine*, II (July, 1955), 65.

[12] Kingsley Amis, "One World and its Way," review of Robert Liddell's *The Novels of I. Compton-Burnett*, *Twentieth Century*, CLVIII (Aug., 1955), 173.

[13] Edward Sackville-West, "Ladies whose bright Pens . . .", chapter VI in *Inclinations* (London, 1949), p. 81.

[14] Henry Reed, *The Novel Since* 1939 (London, 1946), p. 19.

[15] Amis, p. 172.

[16] José Ortega y Gasset, *The Dehumanization of Art and Notes on the Novel*, trans. Helene Weyl (Princeton, 1948), p. 87.

[17] Ibid., p. 65.

[18] I. Compton-Burnett and M. Jourdain, "A Conversation," *Orion: A Miscellany*, I (1945), 25.

[19] Kermode, "House of Fiction," p. 73.

[20] Trans. Eva Le Gallienne, Modern Library College ed. (New York, 1957), p. 227.

CHAPTER III

[1] Peter Grosvenor, "Such moral but wicked people!", interview with I. Compton-Burnett and review of *A God and his Gifts*, *Daily Express*, Nov. 21, 1963.

[2] I. Compton-Burnett and M. Jourdain, "A Conversation," *Orion: A Miscellany*, I (1945), p. 89.

[3] Elizabeth Bowen, "Ivy Compton-Burnett," in *Collected Impressions* (New York, 1950), p. 89.

[4] Frank Kermode, "The House of Fiction: Interviews with Seven English Novelists," *Partisan Review*, XXX (Spring, 1963), 72.

[5] Henri Bergson, *Laughter*, trans. Cloudesley Brereton and Fred Rothwell (London, 1911), p. 21.

[6] Sigmund Freud, "Wit and Its Relation to the Unconscious," in *The Basic Writings of Sigmund Freud* (New York, 1938), p. 634.

CHAPTER IV

[1] Pamela Hansford Johnson, *I. Compton-Burnett* (London, 1951), p. 22.

[2] Richard Strachey, "The Works of Ivy Compton-Burnett," *Life and Letters*, XII (Apr., 1935), 35.

[3] "Aeschylus and Austen," review of *The Mighty and Their Fall*, *The Times Literary Supplement*, Sept. 22, 1961, p. 625.

[4] Edward Sackville-West, "Ladies whose bright Pens . . .", chapter VI in *Inclinations* (London, 1949), p. 88.

[5] "Interview with Miss Compton-Burnett," *Review of English Literature*, III (Oct., 1962), 105, 110.

[6] John Burrows and Alex Hamilton, interview with Joyce Cary, in *Aspects of Fiction*, ed. Howard E. Hugo (Boston, 1962), p. 223.

[7] Raymond Las Vergnas, "Ivy Compton-Burnett," *Revue de Paris*, LXVII (Sept., 1960), 119–120.

CHAPTER V

[1] Trans. Philip Vellacott, Penguin ed. (London, 1956), p. 38.

[2] V. S. Pritchett, "Miss Compton-Burnett," review of Robert Liddell's *The Novels of I. Compton-Burnett*, *New Statesman and Nation*, n.s. XLIX (Mar. 5, 1935), 328.

[3] "Aeschylus and Austen," review of *The Mighty and Their Fall*, *The Times Literary Supplement*, Sept. 22, 1961, p. 625.

CHAPTER VI

[1] "Interview with Miss Compton-Burnett," *Review of English Literature*, III (Oct., 1962), 107.

[2] Angus Wilson, "Ivy Compton-Burnett," review of Robert Liddell's *The Novels of I. Compton-Burnett*, *London Magazine*, II (July, 1955), 68.

[3] José Ortega y Gasset, *The Dehumanization of Art and Notes on the Novel*, trans. Helene Weyl (Princeton, 1948), p. 62.

[4] Pamela Hansford Johnson, *I. Compton-Burnett* (London, 1951), p. 7.

BIBLIOGRAPHY

"Aeschylus and Austen." Review of *The Mighty and Their Fall*. *The Times Literary Supplement*, Sept. 22, 1961, p. 625.

Amis, Kingsley. "One World and its Way." Review of Robert Liddell's *The Novels of I. Compton-Burnett*. *Twentieth Century*, CLVIII (Aug., 1955), 168–175.

"Author and her Aberration, An." Review of *A God and his Gifts*. *The Times Literary Supplement*, Nov. 21, 1963, p. 941.

"Autocrat of the Tea Table, The." Review of *Bullivant and the Lambs* [American title of *Manservant and Maidservant*]. *Time*, LII (July 19, 1948), 112, 114, 116.

Baro, Gene. "With a Shiver and a Laugh." Review of *A God and his Gifts*. *New York Times Book Review*, Feb. 2, 1964, p. 5.

Bland, D. S. "T. S. Eliot's Case-Book." *Modern Language Notes*, LXXV (Jan., 1960), 23–26.

Bogan, Louise. "Childhood's False Eden: I. Compton-Burnett," in *Selected Criticism*. New York, 1955, pp. 189–190.

Bowen, Elizabeth. "Ivy Compton-Burnett," in *Collected Impressions*. New York, 1950, pp. 82–91.

Brooke-Rose, Christine. Review of *A God and his Gifts* [and of Iris Murdoch's *The Unicorn*]. *London Magazine*, n.s. III (March, 1964), 83–86.

Burkhart, Charles. "I. Compton-Burnett: A Note on the Conventions." *Western Review*, XIV (Winter, 1950), 145–148.

"Comic Tragedy." Review of *Brothers and Sisters*. *Time*, LXIX (Jan. 28, 1957), 104, 106.

Compton-Burnett, I., and M. Jourdain. "A Conversation." *Orion: A Miscellany*, I (1945), 20–28.

Cosman, Max. "Manners and Morals." *Commonweal*, LXXI (Feb. 5, 1960), 525–527.

Coxe, Louis O. "A Tyrant's Little World." Review of *Mother and Son*. *New Republic*, CXXXII (Apr. 4, 1955), 18–19.

Crane, Milton. "Dialogue on a Dark Theme." Review of *Brothers and Sisters*. *Saturday Review*, XL (Mar. 2, 1957), 14–15.

Cranston, Maurice. "Ivy Compton-Burnett." [Trans. from the English by Renée Villoteau.] *Lettres Nouvelles*, VI (Oct., 1958), 425–440.

Dunbar, Olivia Howard. "Neglected Novelist." Review of *A Family and a Fortune*. *New Republic*, CII (Apr. 22, 1940), 548–549.

"Extra Grudge Against Life, An." Review of *A God and his Gifts*. *Time*, LXXXIII (Feb. 14, 1964), 100.

"Fact or Fiction?" [Leader.] *The Times Literary Supplement*, Oct. 7, 1960, p. 645.

Fraser, G. S. *The Modern Writer and his World*. London, 1953, pp. 122–123.

Fremantle, Anne. "Tragedy in Teacups." Review of *A Father and his Fate. Saturday Review*, XLI (Apr. 19, 1958), 22–23.

"Futures in the Past." Review of *Two Worlds and Their Ways. Time*, LIII (June 13, 1949), 104.

Gill, Brendan. "Ivy Compton-Burnett and the Gift of Gab." Review of *Manservant and Maidservant. New Yorker*, XXIV (June 19, 1948), 77–78, 81.

Gold, Joseph. "Exit Everybody: The Novels of Ivy Compton-Burnett." *Dalhousie Review*, XLII (Summer, 1962), 227–238.

Greenfield, Stanley B. "'Pastors and Masters': The Spoils of Genius." *Criticism*, II (Winter, 1960), 66–80.

Grosvenor, Peter. "Such moral but wicked people!" Interview with I. Compton-Burnett and review of *A God and his Gifts. Daily Express*, Nov. 21, 1963.

"Hells of Ivy, The." Review of *A Heritage and its History. Time*, LXXV (Feb. 15, 1960), 112, 115.

Horder, Lord. "Glittering Tide of the Peculiar." Review of *A Heritage and its History. Time and Tide*, XL (Oct. 17, 1959), 1134–1135.

"I. Compton-Burnett" [an interview]. *The Times*, Nov. 21, 1963.

"Interview with Miss Compton-Burnett." *Review of English Literature*, III (Oct., 1962), 96–112.

Jefferson, D. W. "A Note on Ivy Compton-Burnett." *Review of English Literature*, I (Apr., 1960), 19–24.

Johnson, Pamela Hansford. *I. Compton-Burnett*. London, 1951.

Johnson, Pamela Hansford. "Three Novelists and the Drawing of Character: C. P. Snow, Joyce Cary and Ivy Compton-Burnett." *Essays and Studies*, n.s. III (1950), 82–99.

Jullian, Philippe. "Thé chez miss Compton-Burnett." *Nouvelles Littéraires*, Mar. 10, 1960, p. 5.

Kermode, Frank. Review of *A Heritage and its History*, in "Fiction Chronicle." *Partisan Review*, XXVII (Summer, 1960), 553–554.

Kermode, Frank. Review of *The Mighty and Their Fall*, in "Fiction Chronicle." *Partisan Review*, XXIX (Summer, 1962), pp. 471–472.

Kermode, Frank. "The House of Fiction: Interviews with Seven English Novelists." *Partisan Review*, XXX (Spring, 1963), 61–82.

Las Vergnas, Raymond. "Ivy Compton-Burnett." *Revue de Paris*, LXVII (Sept., 1960), 114–121.

Liddell, Robert. "The Novels of I. Compton-Burnett," Appendix III in *A Treatise on the Novel*. London, 1947, pp. 146–163.

Liddell, Robert. *The Novels of I. Compton-Burnett*. London, 1955.

McCabe, Bernard. "Ivy Compton-Burnett, An English Eccentric." *Critique* (Univ. of Minnesota), III, no. 2 (1960), 47–63.

Mackworth, Cecily. "Les Romans d'Ivy Compton-Burnett." *Critique* (Paris), XIV (May, 1958), 396–404.

Newby, P. H. "The Art of the Novel: Ivy Compton-Burnett and Henry Green," in *The Novel 1945–1950*. London, 1951, pp. 29–32.

"Of Human Bondage." Review of *Mother and Son*. *Time*, LXV (Apr. 4, 1955), 100.

Prescott, Orville. "Comrades of the Coterie," Chap. VI in *In My Opinion*. Indianapolis, 1952, pp. 92–109.

Preston, John. "'The Matter in a Word.'" Review of *A Heritage and its History*. *Essays in Criticism*, X (July, 1960), 348–356.

Pritchett, V. S. "Miss Compton-Burnett." Review of Robert Liddell's *The Novels of I. Compton-Burnett*. *New Statesman and Nation*, n.s. XLIX (Mar. 5, 1955), 328–329.

Raphael, Frederic. "Never a word too many." Review of *A God and his Gifts*. *Sunday Times*, Nov. 24, 1963.

Reed, Henry. *The Novel Since* 1939. London, 1946, pp. 18–20.

Sackville-West, Edward. "Ladies whose bright Pens . . .", Chap. VI in *Inclinations*. London, 1949, pp. 78–103.

Sarraute, Nathalie. "Conversation et sous-conversation," in *L'Ère du Soupçon*. Paris, 1956, pp. 81–124.

"Series of Delicate Keys, A." Review of *Mother and Son* and of Robert Liddell's *The Novels of I. Compton-Burnett*. *The Times Literary Supplement*, Feb. 11, 1955, p. 88.

Snow, Lotus. "'Good Is Bad Condensed': Ivy Compton-Burnett's View of Human Nature." *Western Humanities Review*, X (Summer, 1956), 271–276.

Strachey, Richard. "The Works of Ivy Compton-Burnett." *Life and Letters*, XII (Apr., 1935), 30–36.

"Vulture and Cat." Review of *Mother and Son*. *Newsweek*, XLV (Apr. 11, 1955), 115–116.

Waugh, Evelyn. "Op. XV." Review of *A Father and his Fate*. *Spectator*, CXCIX (Aug. 16, 1957) 223.

Webster, Harvey Curtis. "A Visit with Ivy Compton-Burnett." *Saturday Review*, XL (Mar. 2, 1957), 14–15.

West, Anthony. "Ivy Compton-Burnett," in *Principles and Persuasions*. New York, 1957, pp. 225–232.

Wilson, Angus. "Ivy Compton-Burnett." Review of Robert Liddell's *The Novels of I. Compton-Burnett*. *London Magazine*, II (July, 1955), 64–70.

Yarling, Bass. "Miss Ivy's Tobacco Road." Review of *Brothers and Sisters*. *New Republic*, CXXXVI (Mar. 4, 1957), 20–21.

INDEX